Cc
IN AN ICON

Francis Patrick Sullivan

Foreword by Burton Raffel

Drawings by Aileen Callahan

ETOILE INTERNATIONAL PRODUCTIONS
2008

Acknowledgments

Much gratitude goes to the following people who helped to make this book a reality:

Burton Raffel for his generous Foreword.
T. Frank Kennedy, S.J. and the Jesuit Community of the Boston College, William B. Neenan, S.J., John Michalczyk, Scott Kinder, Stephen Vedder, Michael Swanson, David Horn, John Atteberry, Lisa Taddeo, Richard Jenson, Xiaxiao Chen, Chuon Nguyen, M.J. Connolly.

A.C.

ISBN number: 978-0-615-25825-6

Cover Design: Michael Swanson

ETOILE INTERNATIONAL PRODUCTIONS 2008

CONTENTS

There were centuries, in English and then American history, when religion was at the very center of life and, inevitably, at the center of most poetry. Deeply secular poets were rare and totally secular poets were nonexistent. By the end of the nineteenth century, however, the situation was reversed, and a very great religious poet, the Jesuit Gerard Manley Hopkins, was far more than a mere anomaly. For three decades after his death in 1889, indeed, he was a non-entity. Even the long delayed publication of *Poems*, in 1918, was anything but an epochal event. The first printing, a modest total of 1,500 copies, was not sold out until 1930. And Hopkins' large reputation, truthfully, remains distinctly more a poetic than a religious triumph.

Francis Sullivan, writing almost a century later, is in many ways the heir to Hopkins' achievement and, less than ten years after his death in 1996, suffers from much the same neglect. *Conversations In An Icon* (a line from which I have made the title to this brief essay) should provide a spur to his reputation. Like Hopkins a Jesuit, and like Hopkins, too, of Celtic ancestry, Francis (as I always addressed him) was emphatically God-centered. But unlike Hopkins, who wove his poetry closely around the theology and events of his priestly existence, Francis reached out to the world and, in a sense, flung his poems to its far corners. Hopkins was often a dour Welshman; Francis, though as profoundly serious as any man I have ever known, was often a cheerful and almost invariably a positive oriented Irishman. Profoundly human love, in all its manifestations, was basic to Francis' theology, to his life, and to his poetry:

It was so painful
to me, those times I begged anything
with a shape to go to you, to tell you
in some tongue-tied pedagogy
of bark, or leaf, or face, or limb, or voice
that a love could come to its rest in you
to honor you, not to make you
incredulous…

Francis' Introduction tells us that the female speaker of these lines is the Holy Spirit, "always 'she'…[and]manifest[ing] the constant urgency to create new forms, especially when forms have fragmented." This vision of the Holy Spirit, he tells us, will – like the figure of Jesus, in this long poem – "often...tell narratives which seem not to come to theological conclusion." That is very much Francis' way, as it seems to me to be our time's way. It is without question not the way of Gerard Manley Hopkins. A voice that is probably Francis' own says, in *Conversations In An Icon*, "When I am opened this way, / Too much pours in." This is not the voice of fully settled doctrine, of theology firmly and fixedly planted. It is groping, all too human, and as all inclusive as one man, one priest, one poet can make it.

> Love...is unstoppable. Maybe I live
> with small names, so have
> felt some unstoppables. But when
> someone says your name, and
> the name is right, a wonderful set
> of mountains, a sky , a sea,
> and a crowd fill space.

And the Holy Spirit assures Jesus, who in this brave, gestational poem is never less than himself or than the man he also was, "That I never wanted you to be anyone else, / not a god, not a form, not a face, than yours."
This is what Francis strove all his life to tell everyone who would listen. "God is not lonely, god is livid pain / or livid joy with everyone laying it on." There are joyous moments in this fine poem, as there are sad ones, even raucous ones. There is crisp dialogue, and immense lyrical tenderness, all supplemented by Aileen Callahan's stark insightful illustrations. *Conversations In An Icon* is neither a treatise nor in any way a substitute for other religious writing. "To return someone to themselves is the effect of true creativity, of true beauty, " Francis writes toward the close of his Introduction. In this until now unpublished poem he set himself exactly that task, and he has performed it as only he could.

Burton Raffel
Professor of Arts and Humanities Emeritus
University of Louisiana at Lafayette

INTRODUCTION

Conversations In An Icon is a fiction out looking for a truth. As Andre Rublev's Holy Trinity Icon is a fiction out looking for the truth of a Christian doctrine. A fought over doctrine. A doctrine still tenuous in some modern biblical inquiry. But one intensely attractive to the artistic mind, and to my poetic one. Which, sees in a kind of Christianity an incorrigible bias toward symbolization, making the invisible visible, then holding to the visible, sure that if it is let go, the invisible goes too. Though symbolizing, Christianity stays keenly cautious about idolatry *and* its converse, exploitation, as in disrespectful approaches to the materials of creativity, which is a sort of hatred.

My fiction, built upon Rublev's fiction, which is built upon a doctrinal fiction, which is built upon an interpretation of bible, wants to detect the presence of the believed-in Trinity to contemporary experience by using a poetic sense of contemporary experience, and moving the believed-in Trinity into the contemporary experience as participant, no, not as participant so much, but as the one(s) who experiences the whole. The massive passion and ecstasy of the whole contemporary experience require someone(s) with infinite emotional capability. And someone(s) who cherishes freedom in an infinite way. And. who cherishes autonomy in an infinite way. And union. And harmony. Someone(s) who can prize each unique reality, personal or not, for itself. Someone(s) in whom there is a hope that humankind will always relate with its senses to divinity or humanity. It is my fear that the extinction of sense knowledge will extinguish humanity and divinity both.

My fiction has many voices to it. Four main ones. The three of Rublev's Icon, the angel of the center being the Father, the angel on the viewers right, the Holy Spirit and always "she," the angel on the left the Son of God, Jesus. Since the focal point of an Icon is in front of it where a viewer or prayer may stand or kneel, that focal point is the place of my voice, and of impersonal voices which slide into the "Conversations," and of voices which are indeterminate. Each conversation begins with a designation of who is speaking.

There may be some confusion about the two "he" voices. The "he" of the Father is generally the voice of the one in whom the experience of everything arrives, as everything has gone out from this central figure. As if "he" in a special way undergoes the passion and the ecstasy of the whole. The "he" of the son is generally the voice that comes upon the fragmentations of experience, with this quality apparent, "he" wishes not to lose any of the fragments. The "she" voice manifests the constant urgency to create new forms, especially where forms have been fragmented. All three voices, at various stages of the poem, are able to manifest total appreciation of creation, in whatever stage it is, as autonomous and unconditionally its own. All three voices are lovers of that creation, and ask, through love, to share autonomies with it. Each of the three can speak the others' parts.

When the impersonal, or indeterminate voices enter, they represent those human experiences which have had to endure, destructively or creatively, without any sense of divinity. They are in this fiction to show that large areas of human experience or of a human sense of God lie outside a theologian's or a poet's ability to understand. These areas may not be left silent, however. Often the "he" voices and the "she" voice will tell narratives which seem not to come to theological conclusion. Such a fiction implies in divinity a respect for those who "fable and miss." The essence of what each voice says is written out at the end of the text, under corresponding numbers.

Conversations In An Icon intends no instruction, nor direction, concerning contemporary spiritual life. It contains no abstractable catch phrases. My fiction wants to be itself so much that anyone who reads it might just want to be him or herself and begin a colloquy with other voices, which colloquy will be unique. Not outside of time, nor outside of history. To return someone to themselves is the effect of true creativity, of true beauty, not to a bank vault self, but to a larder self. Creation and Redemption do this. Therefore, a poet's fiction can imitate, from its great distance, and try to do the same.

Francis Patrick Sullivan

THE DRAWINGS

Drawing inside an icon is, for the visual artist, drawing in a dynamic stasis containing endless entry. It is a frontal opening mysteriously lit and shadowed. It is an expanding portal.

Frank Sullivan said to me that in *Conversations In An Icon*, " the text's thrust is the inclusion of the world in the conversation of the Trinity and the inclusion of the Trinity in the conversation of the world. The fourth voice represents the materials of the world given a voice, the impersonal of the world made personal, the elements, the anonymous histories, legends and whatever voice does not have a name."

This collaboration of text and drawings began with Frank Sullivan's poetic manuscript for which the drawings were created. Rather than illustrate the text, the drawings hold a succession of images projected as a visual pulse of the specific text passage. The image form of the drawings is open--relating to places "under" and "within" the written line. The text and drawings enter each other and act upon each other in a dialogue as the viewer participates in the piece. These conversations *in* an icon called for a drawing medium in which deep layered darks and lines with softened edge could gather a tonal "atmosphere" corresponding to the text's psychological states. The velvety chalk black charcoal textures allows the filtering of light in an ambiguous icon space which is knowable and unknowable.

Each voice has a visual motif which is recognized when it appears with a new portion of its text as the "conversation" continues. The following motifs are found within the drawings:

The drawings derive their presence from ideas, movements, shades, relations and dynamics within the poetic written lines. The Father's motif,"I said,"is a plunging vertical which is directed to a V shape. This voice is never a pronouncement and therefore never terminates. The image appears in drawing #24 as a smoldering re-creation following the text's, "recreated at every moment." An upward lift in the image emanates from the text's, "dark center." The "He said" or Son voice of drawing #22 suggests a landscape—a sighting for the "blue-black desert" of the text. Light falls "into" and "on" the recurring arc of this, voice--the arc an element of ascent and return. The rounded form of the "She said" voice of the Holy Spirit expands and contracts from within itself. It holds the convex and concave of its fertility. Drawing # 19 relates to its text, "like something poured" and "there was no emptiness," as a drawing whose focused darkness is abundant and open. The upstretched form of the "It was said" anonymous voice of culture is a gesture motif lit in the drawings from many points and resolved beyond its edges. In drawing #14, appearing to shed itself, the splayed image reflects the lines, "the dream is a crucifixion on white paper, the dream is a holocaust on white paper." Created from the text and autonomous, the drawings function as a prism through which words pass and return again. From the volume light of charcoal they form further configurations and meanings in the "space" where text and drawing speak to each other.

Aileen Callahan

I RANSOM

she said: When you asked me,
it was too late. I could do some rectifying,
make a crutch of a branch,
or sing a cliché that the moon in quarters
was a sail on our ship to the stars
and it had its own wind.
But you have seen recent digs.
Not all the axeheads were for ritual wars.
I was sometimes driven to savagery myself
by the threats of genitals pumping me,
and by being scalped out of my sex.
I have felt the eyes of the dying
crawl upwards into my womb
as if into a temple just ransacked,
and then ask the gods in whispers, "Come back!"
I did not know then gods were there for them.   #1
They were not for me.
But I loved. them. As I loved those fields
that popped like grease in the sun
or had winds across them like a game.
I used to dress in purple mountains,
or come down cliffs in tumbling water,
or be capricious fogs, like tidal waves,
like cavalry. There was an elephant musth got loose
in the men. Have you seen great trees
go down under their violence?
They can hear no song then,
nor see beauty, You see why I can
only make new forms
with any heart. This white flower
was gold. It took years.   It grows
beside the gold as half an earth.
These are not day and night crawling into
each others wombs after gods.

he said: When I saw the face I loved
vanish, I knew an ending to my life,

1

1 I did not know then gods were there

and knew, and knew. That is the truest
death. As the truest life is that face
for me. As I am made by it. I know it.
It is my face and never mine.
When the face I loved vanished that time,
I looked around me in my death
and saw the others empty to the throat,
and then almost an amnesia suffused
them and the weathers of passion
came on and even my death lost
its poignancy. My loss-was-a trifle
in this pity of ravagement. I do
not know what he spared me
when he vanished. He seemed to spare
them nothing. Yet I knew it was
grief, and unbearable grief that turned
him. I never knew such love,   #2
that it could not bear itself in a
faithlessness. And I was left
with his face. As if I could hear him
pleading. But my face was his plea.
To Them. And there were the ravagements.
Some softened when they saw me.
And I was in my death. I do not know
what they saw, but they loved me.
And some killed me. I do not know
if they could see I was already dead
with him vanished. I am speaking of
my body. You know it. It does not go
from your mind. Someone's love can go.
Then there is no face in your mind.
 Someone's love can come back, then
the air is filled with faces, each one different.
It is the body's time when love returns.

she said: What are you free of
if you want new life? I went over
a battleground afterwards and cried out
I will gestate new men, so I found
a shellshocked man and he loved me
and I cared for him and the manchild.

2 I never knew such love

They spoke in quiet gibberish
to each other, and loved each other
for it, and the man gave out his story.
The manchild got up from him
one day of the story and looked at me,
the blood of innocence in his eyes.
He loved me as well, and it pained
him to think I had brought him into
the rhythm of revenge. I should have
left the man to his seed. He made
his weapon and went from the two of us.
He is dead. Or someone else is.
Now you walk on that ground.
You look at a body with no life to it.
If you are a man, see the dead woman.
It ought not to be. Would you not
take her chattering daughter? Would
you not hope that a new innocence
would never comprehend her later
when she tried to say what she saw?
And when her daughter made her weapon
and went from the two of you
and someone would be dead, or she,
what act would you obliterate,
given the chance? There are evenings
I walk up through the gorse   #3
to the purple color of the wind's sky
as it sings to the restless surf,
and I feel the fierce truth coming
off the stench of the dead seaweed
that one more life will stop
one more death. The truth clings to me
as this gown, this sterile lover
not equipped but with feeling and foolishness
like some cub, some evening
all seduction but knowing its impotence
telling me the truth.
There are only the shellshocked men
or the chattering girls. And one other.
The one in full self-possession seducing
the one who is not. To make a new
innocence. To have a motive

5

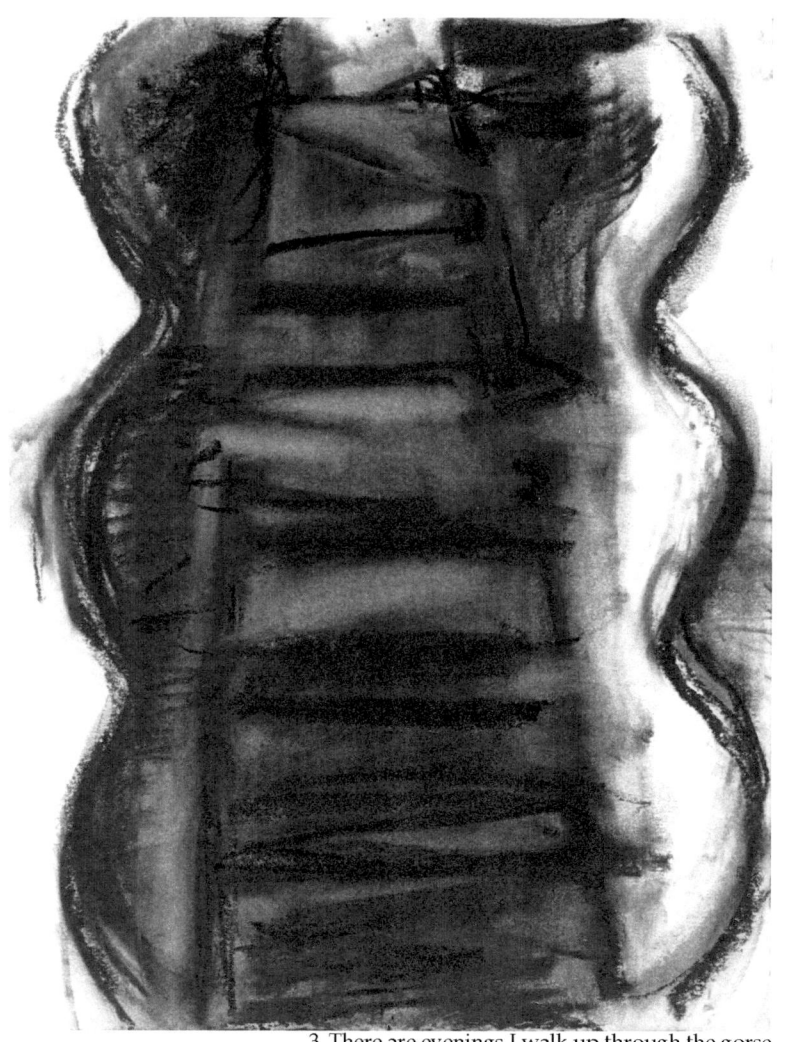

3 There are evenings I walk up through the gorse

that will not be judged guilty by him
or her who is born and hears the story.
Do you know this judgment?
The woman who sang sailors onto her reef?
The man who sang 'maidens onto his fire?
Stories. But I have seen it in
the eyes of someone who loved me,
as though I had put a fox inside his
throat to eat his never enough flesh,
and he must find other flesh, or be it.
The same who knew the purple evening
I had shown him, and the great
gorse ringing out its silences,
and the promise of the sea to return always,
who clung to me like a gown.
But oh! that moment of clean flesh,
when nothing more than love is possible,
and nothing fits in its hand but you,
and nothing in its mouth but you,
and its father is empty of his shellfire
memories and sees the fields of before.
It is a vanishing truth. like an evening.
It has me mad with itself.

she said: I never wanted you to be
anyone else. I once showed you a calico shell
with a helix turban and the mouth of a sousaphone,
and you thought it was something else,
a vagina I was promising, or a horn for a war.
The shell was its own form. I could meet you
in that shell, but its calico and helix
held their space and their time. As you do. As I.
It can never know how much I love it.   #4
Nor any form.   The aluminum vestal crouched
over a copper flame on a pedestal in a fountain.
But you can. Know how much I love it,
any form, in its insensibility. But its
self hold on space and time. Know how much
I love you. But you will have to guess it.
You will be in total-charge-that way.
Reading the calico shell I love, the small thunder

4 You can know how much I love it, any form

the vivid silver when the mist comes up
from the water to the sun in the early afternoon.
Reading that I am mesmerized by faces,
that a crowd is a despair because I cannot
see all its faces. Reading that I know all
the deaths, that I am like an ashtray
full of the stubs of them. Oh, some of the deaths!
I have no sanity in them. And as if I
cannot die and am pinned to watch them,
pinned to insanity. Those times I have
harbored this shell, its climb, its pure
calico like an innocence unheard of,
as if it had taken a madhouse and spun it like
a top and in the blur the craze was cured.
You will read that I know all the lives.
That I never wanted you to be anyone else,
not a god, not a form, not a face, than yours.

he said: Outcomes occur in a small space,
the fates of spring cactuses, of an indigo bunting,
of loves, of hates. You know this
if you've waited for a call, or for a bird.
Or the words to come to the concentration
of you in the single place where, if it is love
coming, there is the ineradicable spot of you,
the ruby throat, and if it is not, there is
that death you wear the way jews wore
their death in a star. You are a target,   #5
not visible. Not necessary to be for love
or hate. You create the place. Where they
may come. You own vulnerability.
If you love the fire whisks of sunset,
the night will be a cold love in that place.
When there is an outcome, it spreads
from the place and you are a bird of fire,
or a flame pinched out by thumb and finger,
or both. Love and hate might be this snow
at night. Arriving on your face with no
alternation. The burn of the cold.
The dream of the freezing. Spreading in you.

5 You are a target, not visible

She was left on my doorstep with a note
pinned to her skin, "Not Your Kind Here!"
With him, it was just the note. "You will
find him somewhere." "Burn This And You
Will Know Where To Get Him! " They were a star.
And a ruby, and I was a bird of fire
from them and I wore a gold. death from
them, and that is the outcome for me.
To which these murders have come. Into
the same space. Spreading in me as they
did. As the flights of bunting, of hummingbirds.
As the whisks of clouds. As ephemeral cactuses.
As snow, and nightfall currycombed to sleep.

he said When I had failed, I left my songs,   #6
as you would leave scribblings carelessly in a room.
I sat in the shadow of a wall still warm from the sun,
and let it soothe me so long as it was silent.
Then I heard the singing of a woman's voice,
not a song I knew, but I knew every word of it,
my own words, the ones that had died in my mouth:
god can say with rain his love, /with dust, the sins he knows /
god can say his mind with a rose /with dust, what he must love //
I can say my love with dust /dance it for the wind, /
I can say with god my mind, /dance it for the dust //
she can light a sky of blue, /wear it as red hair, /
god can get his fire from her, /I, my dance of blue. //
We can say with dust our love. /We can say it knows /
our mind dances in a rose, /on fire with our blue love. /
I began to speak to her in the secrecy of myself,
as if I were fitting pottery pieces together to guess design.
There is a cold fury to the focus of men and women.
It happens when they are asked to be space and time,
and not a silence and an emptiness.
I have felt life and death fluctuate inside me,
the way tall grass heads move with their shadows on sand,
the one as lovely as the other, as if they were separable,
and I reached for the shadow to laugh at myself.
And there was the sand with its warm shadow.
Then nothing was separable. She must hear my secrecy.
The silence of me gone. I have felt god had great speech.

11

6 When I had failed, I left my songs

Which gave me speech, shadows of the grass kind,
shadows of the sand kind, laugh at itself,
but sudden, and through cracks like dust
or light red from the gone sun, saying nothing is
separable. There is a blue dance and a black dance.
And love is something. that goes through you, keeps time,
that woman singing, she must be love, she knows
what the design was of the broken pot.

II   RISK

he said: Each eater is eaten, or nearly--
the earth eats humans. Death is death only
in the survivor. At the edge of his imagination.
Even now the whole drama is played on that edge.
The blur of the panther, of the cheetah,
the pelican aligning a fish for its throat,
the massacre of anyone, near any river, begins
itself, after itself, in his consciouness
who knows what the dead do not:
his is the glass-like sensitivity smashed
in the hurting sounds and sights.
He knows the death of the deer, who eats
its meat, if he wishes, if some why forms
its cloud at the edge of him,
and strikes its lightning several places
on the expanse of grass and wind he knows is
his life. As if he walked into
the camp of the massacred and they were
carcasses to be left to night prowlers and to birds,
then saw something alive just born
still on her string and their it too went,
and his memory, against his will,
took time past and with its brushes
made alive every instant-of the raid,
and he became-each one where he or she

7 And he knew the place of death

fell and how, and each feeling, from
terror to sleep to forgetting to easing
and he knew the place of death was in   #7
the living mind, the place of stars
shaken loose and falling in bloody streaks
you could smell was in the living mind,
the place where all the physical agonies
rose up in flocks, endless upsweeps, cries,
blocking out the sun, was in the living mind,
there in that small space alone could it be.
As if one moment held every moment,
and one mind knew the one every moment.
They will come and present me all their deaths,
the man said. The world eating the world
will present itself to me if I stay living.
Then the great cracking trees. Then the rampaging
rivers. Then the surf of fires across prairies.
The man stood up from the massacre.
He saw the tracks leading out from the bowl,
and the exultation of the victors crept to
and the cry of their children crept to
the edge of his mind. He saw their women lie down
under them and it was love, and terror
crept to the edge of his mind. He saw them
lie down in their graves in peace, and
fear crept to the edge of his mind. He saw them.
He sat down again in the massacre,
and he saw the last lives on the earth except
his own, he saw how someone ends,
how there can be a last gold anemone,
a last wisp of a thunderhead,
a last red rim of a sun, below the
teeth of the breasts of far, far mountains,
and quiet came to the edge of his mind.
Then he looked straight up into the blue sky.
Then he stood up and lay the blue sky
over them, and he imagined their dance,
and he danced in their place slow and wheeling
like a hawk, and at the edge
of his mind they rose below the blue sky,
and they went on to where they were going.

8 Even as you think killing is the cause of life

he said: Even as you think killing
sketches floral patterns, white ink on
blue matting. She has finished mountains
with rust borders, and more northerly ones
with green sawtooth edges forbidding
sky any trespass. She is doing ferns in
white ram's horn. She has finished shadows
under desert rocks, left them breathing
imperceptibly as shallow water fish
trapped in tidal pools. Even as you think   #8
killing is the cause of life, she has taken
a gray pencil and put in laughing gulls,
then a green, and the sea is scalloped.
Then she removes the copper color of a tall
building and sets a copper block under
the corner of a sky to keep it from tilting
and spilling its hardware on the asphalt.
Then she cuts in half a diesel engine,
and twists the shaft, and the larynxes
move up and down in wordless monologue.
Then she slows music in bubbles from
a soap ring and they collide with plate
glass in an unsmash smash you feel.
"love is nowhere, going nowhere, hunter;
understand, and set your weapon near
a rock, and walk no tracks to nowhere.
love is somewhere, going somewhere, woman,
understand, and set your game near
a bush, and watch love come from somewhere.
everywhere without a kill, love leaves
tracks to nowhere. everywhere without a
trace, love will come from somewhere."
When she finishes she goes back to the sky.
Even as you think again killing is the cause
of life, a man stands up in the sky,
unscrews a rainbow and whirls its tube
so all four notes fill every open space,
and teeth chatter in sympathy to the
rainbow swung like a snake by the tail.
Then he sits down and he speaks:
"I know this mirage is like all beauty.
It seems to be a life lifted from death,
earth colors painted on glass and the rain
comes and makes it its own mockery,
it seems to be someone vanishing out the door,
it is more lake someone coming you did not

17

expect, someone who knows you, you can
tell by the questions, as if you had been
tasted, as if you were a wine that pleased.
It may be just a color, but it comes,
there are no splotches of blood on it,
it is not a hide laid across your lap,
it is not a girl's skin worn by a priest.
There is the sky from which it was taken
still eternal in dignity and in council
When it is gone, you may hear the tears
of things. It is always going. As if
it feared for itself. As if it knew that
death brought nothing. That if it died,
what was not itself would vanish into
catatonia without a vision of itself.
As if it knew it must remain mirage."
When he finishes, he stands and goes back
into the sky. Then the man and woman
are not there any more. Even as you know
killing is not the cause of life in you.

she said: It is as the plunge into sex,
that plunge into another, it is no flying,
this love, yes, it can rifle fire,
multiplied collisions in a fog,
and flames taking their toil,
it can be the lie that winds the clock-
spring too tight into freezing, no it is
not outside itself, it is a plunge into
another, as into terminal darknesses
along with someone to those borders,
as into justices with arms locked,
yes, it is a horde, yes, it is alone
waving truce with a white kerchief,
it is carnal each way,
it is a plunge into carnality,
it is no plunge away,
it is the great compassion spoken,
or the great dispassion, that
which is left unsaid at the mouth
of the oven, at the two steps frontwards
for the accused. It is carnal, love
is a plunge into carnality,
it has no rules, it has no need

of passport, it may not be taxed,
it is cursed, it is blessed, it is
in itself neither curse nor blessing,
it is compassion, it is mercy's.
parent, it is a parent of paradise,
it is the shadow of every hell,
this plunge into the flesh.
I have been in my space
when a sword made a shriek near it,
when limitless snow fell through
my lamplight and would not speak
its wish, I have been there
and heard bullets whine at me,
but I have been there when the rain
was green on everything, and when
a flute played to itself, or a voice sang
someone dead back to life,
I have been there when someone has come
full of love as a bin of apples
tumbled out on a wood floor for the blind
who could hear their color and juice.
Love is different every time,
it is a different plunge each time,
it is a different compassion,
it is a scenario of skies, free flesh
mixed with animals and fowl and
brass choirs and the dark regimes
of birthing, and the light regimes
of dying, as if there were copulations
in a waterfall, or justice itself
on the bench at sundown, or mercy
itself raising up from sleep mornings,
and there are the ascetics marching

away as pines down the slopes out
to the desert where they will be tempted
fiercely to turn into twisted sculpture
with untouchable beauty,
up the slopes as pines as if
they were rising from the dead into
a bridegroom blue without a
horizon to his name and poor to
the bone clouds of his carnality.

she said: When I told you I loved you,
you looked to see what you wore to make it so.
You turned blank page after blank page.
You thought it was a girl and looked in a mirror
to be sure of your face. You thought a woman
would drink only a matured brew,
or that I was but some pulse that came blindly,
as directed by some decision so as to use you
for a prism, but with delight
in the beginning to engage you in a contract
whose delight would fade when the last
words were chiseled into the stone
of agreement. You would be the prism
the instructor would use to show how light was
not sound to a peeking audience.
I was the pencil flash directed through you.
It is not so, this. It was so painful
to me, those times I begged anything
with a shape to go to you, to tell you
in some tongue-tied pedagogy
of bark, or leaf, or face, or limb, or voice
that a love could come to its rest in you
to honor you, not to make you
incredulous, a victorian butler in his
master's smoking jacket, or someone
who could never be known, and so, loved
for some other reason, some outside reason,
face, or use, or acquisition.
You would never let my love sail in on you,
a word sound of a horn's music
or that flute/soprano mad song, so
un-mad, in its calculated random notes,
a whole world could fit inside it
even to the butterfly pursued by a bird,
even to the hideous causes of war
being explained with cool reason to a mob.
I will say it to you again.
I love you for what I know. Where you stand.
Whatever the weather. Whatever the flak of words
or the quick motion of your eyes sorting
out the crowd for similes. Or for companions.
It has made a difference in my life.
I may not enter yours.
But I may see it, not just in its willow
switches, but in its larger gestures
during the times you thought no one knew,

so you thought it better not to know
yourself and to be the ticker typing averages
from a Wall Street on some corner tongue.
When I was loved, it was too much to hold.
Yet whom could I tell except him
who loved me. I could tell everyone!
I almost did. But in the telling, something
happened that stretched me as wide as
any two arms can stretch. I fell in love   #9
again and again and again, it was as if
everything came to me for a new name,
a name which would unlock their tongues,
and I could only give the name
if I knew their speech, and there were
the flowers, and the great droves of birds,
and there were the hoarse cities
with their frozen ears outsized, listening,
and there you were too, and I
gave you a name you have almost
forgotten, as you have almost forgotten
your own heart. It only comes back to you
when in the space where nothing exists,
you put a word that sings to itself,
and you stand back and hear it,
and you sense that I can hear it,

9 I fell in love again and again and again

then a crowd comes, and you hear only the crowd;

he said: A man took teakwood
and carved a penis with it. With sandalwood
he made wings to attach to the base
of the teak penis. With the same wood
he made waves out of which
it flew. He took teak again and carved
angelic and demonic faces circling
the emergence of this god. There was
no more wood, so god was complete.
There was no more wood. No one
saw it was wood. There was only god.
I can tell you the same story of vaginas,
the same of androgynies, the same
of the dancer, of the old man of the sky.
I may use bronze. Then, there is
no more bronze; words, and there are
no more words, only the god.
I may sit there and burn the penis
and its colleagues to a fine ash,
set it in my palm and blow it
into your eyes and breath to make
a minor chaos in your belief. Or
melt the bronze into a valourous medal
to strengthen your disbelief. So,
the spaces are no salvations except
for the deaf and dumb. "*There was a man
who had a tree planted the day he
was born to be his constant prayer,
The man grew to an age beyond number,
and the tree expressed every prayer.
He had only to come to it and be silent
with his hands placed on what it said.
He came onetime after a journey
and it was gone, though its fresh
dust and stoppered roots were there.
He went to the priests and asked them
where it was gone and they showed
him what they had carved from its
fine wood, and set in the sanctuary.
He said, is it their prayer? They said it was.
He offered a respect to them and went
back to the empty space, and found a seed*

of that tree pressed down by a foot,
unharmed in the print, so he sat on the
stump and he listened for a long while,
the end of life itself sitting on an empty tree.
When he had news of the day's one birth,
he got up and left his prayer forever,
but went close by, near where other trees
were growing, and in a patch of light
he planted a new tree as the prayer of
the new child and told no one of it.
He sat there to watch it grow. He was
found there. They put him among the tombs
saying no one should have touched
his prayer tree.   He had nothing to leave
to the future, so he died into the past,
But he knew they had to touch his prayer
tree. He knew his prayers were no more
in it. Yet it was their prayer. He
knew that empty space was empty prayer,
so he linked a new life to a" new-seed."
I could burn it to ashes and blow it
in your face. And that empty space
would be the deaf and dumb begging
you, and you would give food to their
gibberish, and they would die of grief.
And that would be a space you could not fill.
So you must go and cut a new tree.

I said: When I am opened this way,
too much pours in. A pole of larkspur
with too many bees, or a clock tower right
in the sun. I see the bargaining over dreams.
What vulnerability the human future has!
Triage for its ideal! . The old world--well,--lost—
for--love nostrum burning atop a gas pipe
in a white desert sun. As if it says love
into a perplexity, as if it is saying to
the bottom of a well, ring, ring, rise
to the sun and roll its barrel down, adown!
Silliness! But passion accumulates
in small grains in me. As if I hit a toe
in the dark, and danced, then barked
a shin, and laughed to make sense,
laughed at my instinctive blasphemies
and intentions of revenge, and at my pity.

Helplessness! You do not know this.
You can stand in the welter of passion
and not laugh. As if pure colors arose
from your hands and you absorbed each
like absorbing fire, or swallowing swords,
but then the spectacular evanesces,
and you pass a hat and I can smell
your sweat, the putrefaction of your clothes,
and I keep on walking with histories
dealing themselves out onto my mind
of what you know where you stay.
Because I love charm. I think of it   #10
when I plot futures for history and for time,
not just my own. Though I stop when
I think of the camps. I am total silence
when a man tells of them. I let him draw
any future in space, however terrifying,
as if he owned unfilled time whose
filled time was anti-time.
It comes down like a kite. He pulls,
but it heads itself in eights into the ground.
I am useless with burned loves. I can
look at melted skin and the eyes caught
in it, but I am a fire, and I know
behind the eyes there is a fear not mortal.
I read about them. I say to my soul,
be compassionate! If they knew you were,
they would be enraged you did nothing,
or would know you couldn't, and they would
have mercy on you, and no death smaller.
And you would know the death they could not.
And it happens again. Compassion gets blown
off by a gust, and its sheets separate, catch
loosely on bushes, then blow off further, like
memories of things too personal.

10   Because I love charm

I write a letter. I speak passionately.
I spend years putting a vision together,
small, but powerful. It is printed.
It disappears. I'm back to the stubbed toe
and the blasphemies in the dark, the laugh!
To the dream of charm! Which you understand.
Not colors, but birds rising from your hand,
flying free out over the audience afraid
of their droppings, pouters, shuttlecocks,
speedy sparrows, huge flapping crows
that raise the laughter level, a condor
who flops on stage and snores still asleep
from inside your coat, an unbudging owl,
then clap, clap, and they all fly back,
line up beside you seriously and bow,
then split left and right and are gone!
This is no betrayal. It is the dream I bargain
with when my compassion is blown off!

I said: I thought she chewed her foot off
to get free of the trap, but she kept eating
her foot, then she found out her heart tasted
better, then she swallowed her tongue and
flipped her eyes after it, shuddered, and I
stopped imagining what she was doing to
herself with that narcissistic self-preserving,
and ascribed it all to the consuming darkness
self-love is before it eats a strange light
and turns into soft darkness
that will set a rose before you in a glass
carafe so breakfast will sing for the two of` you.
I had to pull my hand out of her mouth
before this happened. I had tried to
save her tongue and catch her eyes, her
last pair of dice. It was not my dream that
bargained. But I knew the winning dream,
I knew when I saw the total darkness
turn warm right before my eyes,
that the light, the one that had switched me,
was there, but had been taken in,
and there was the rose in the glass carafe,
and here is the paradox full shot,
she was clear as the glass and the rose
who was filled with warm darkness.

But there is another who burns like the sun
right at the center, and I keep feeding
cloth into her, not a silk moth sun and
plaid mulberry leaves that will yield
bolts of silk already shot, but a crucible-
like self to whom everything is dross
unless it is white hot, unseeable,
unvisitable, except in morning or evening
arguments, eden's god stuck overhead
in its own decrees, and snow kings below
unable to raise their hands for mercy,
several pities staring at one another briefly,
then one pity staring by itself. Another
inspects glassware for flaws and every glass
is flawed, is broken, and the next is
inspected, and the blowers blow the golden
gob and press it a form, and blow,
put tweezers in its mouth and spin the
tube and there is a purple glass or a pink,
flawed off the end of the tube and pitched
in the pile and on and on the blowing goes,
and there is music to the breakage.
If I made the sun the moon I would have
my dream. And I would be mushroom pale.
If I made flawless glass, she would die,
a vine whose toots were cut along the wall,
left a clinging, brown display of veins
I would have to pull free string by string.
I have dreamed of resurrections since my
obliterated time. Not seasonal. Not
jack-in-the-box sorts that hit you like a
tranquilizing dart, then someone marks your
ear to follow your habits with a bleeper.
Like something coming to itself, like someone
in a tragic coma who clears and says
your name and you know he has himself
and has the past time that put you together.
As if a frightened Lazarus asked for a drink,

11 A few bodies make it into abstraction

saying, let's get out of here, I know a place!
But I do not mean reversals of conditions,
miracle leaps that charm you and send you
out for a drink. I mean the woman who was
the fox is the woman who makes the beauty,
the woman who was the sun is the woman
who weaves the plaid, and the woman who broke
the glass is the woman who glows with music.

it was said: A few bodies make it into   #11
the abstraction. Shamans say they saw some
in nests outside re-growing, where the souls go.
Visionaries walk beside themselves and
are not part and whole. The dead are somewhere.
Their bodies are somewhere discernible.
A few made it into a new physics.
Some say there is a hunger in separate spirits
for their broken molds, the molds on exhibit
showing the rise of humans. Think if they
were to leap to themselves out of the glass,
ape against man, heathen against faithful,
lust between early and late forms,
language rubbing against language is flint
on skin. Souls have equal bafflement,
as they do when living, when they migrate elsewhere,
their long for their old mountains and keen winds,
the comfort of their own soup and cloth.
Nothing can live except this moment,
which is like the flash of an atomic blast;
death is the sound arriving much later.
It is so with a god, it must be, is the light
not sound of the blast.   No time can live
with another time. One must be dead to
live with another, to receive its life from it,
but old time must never know the new time
or there will be a death more painful
than the first. If you sucked a spirit from
Etruscan stone and set it roaming in
heavy auto traffic, this would be a new death.
It cannot be that spirits-watch a time
after their own time, watch whole histories.

12 It would be as if a living being

That is too much to imagine, unless some
physicality remains to them. Then they will
never see beyond their own cloth and soup.
And they are few who made it there.
It would be as if a living being presently   #12
could take in every moment up to now,
not numbers, or measures, but the passions,
the way one would glimpse a valley
or watch carnival from an ironwork balcony,
or be in the sea in a storm or among trees
when the flash of autumn hit it.   The circuit
would break. The living being would curl
into a fetal position and cancel time.
Though there would be dreams of warmth
and solitude, walks on gravel paths
between roses in the splash presence of
fountains and preening birds, the blue sky, cut
in a square and pegged to four gargoyle corners.
Suppose the dam burst that held the dead back
and their stories, and the flood of them
sluiced between the mountains of a living being
set off with gravity to the sea, that would
cause infinite insanity, or a compassion
that could never be broken, one of oceanic
tears, of gale force laughter, with the
attention of the noon sun, as if each emotion
were the fire ball of a killer blast, and the
living being must live in the middle of it,
it being joy and sorrow fully each time.
Time is a desperate flight from its own memory, #13
the blast; it can live out ahead of itself.
If it turns and walks back to itself,
it broaches with too much. The conditions
for eternal life are severe. If the visions
are to substantiate their claims. In a body,
a spirit of anytime. With itself.   If it hates
or loves, it must do so infinitely.
Or be eddy pools the sun dries quickly.

13 Time is a desperate flight

III REPRISAL

it was said: The poet wrote with a stub pencil   #14
on a wrapper: The Thief came out of the sun early
when the eden carpets still dried their rainbows.
He rolled them into dull periques and smoked them.
He has not escaped. He is now smoking dull flowers.
They came, and he ate the wrapper, but they
saw the pencil, so they burned it, and locked him
in a wordless place. Then they said, spread
each dream of yours before us on this table or
we will kill her for your own good. He spread
his dream of her he loved. She was naming furrows in
a new ploughed field purple sleep. She was putting
the sun into a single dish as she would sweep
berries from a table with her hand. She was
drying the heavens on a long line, watching them
wrinkle in the wind and she wrote down auguries:
"out of each flower will come a virtue if you
do not pick them too soon." They took out erasers
and worked, then blew away the grains and said,
store this cleaned sheet under your cot until
we tell you. Then he spread this dream of him
he loved. He was drawing a line in the empty
space between birth and death. He made a gap
unexpectedly and out flew two butterflies who
pursued each other in a fierce search for a
landing place which could only be the other or
each would die of fatigue. So he made a
double loop and two tangents, and there was
a town. So the butterflies had offspring
that filled the town with every colored
wing the world has ever known immortally.
They erased the dream, and he placed the cleaned
sheet under his cot. Then tears of rage rose
up in him and they knew they were close to freeing
him. He spread this dream of himself,
taking wild flowers from the edge of a wheat field,
and walking off with daisies, black eyed susans,
and poppies and queen anne's lace to a clearing
where a soft-eyed deer looked at him and he
threw the flowers like spikes at the deer
and it raced away in wild, wild fear, and
the fields withered and cracked like ancient skin.
They worked quickly and handed him back

14 The poet wrote with a stub pencil

a cleaned sheet and told him, we will
come soon and you will fill the three sheets
with a new dream, one each for the old,
and if you do this we will not kill her for your
own good. He spread the sheets before him
in preparation, then sat still to wait for new
dreams that would not cause her death for him.
But a bluebird had no place to land,
and he filled up with tears and rage and sat
stiff as icon holiness until he broke and in a
twitch put down a branch where it settled.
Then snow began falling down, then up, then
down, as in mad wards the pitiful insane
can find no bench, so in a rage of grief he drew
three bent stalks of grass and the snow rested
like delicious caterpillars on the wind's shoulder.
Then she was blind and walking into space
where she would fall forever, so he put down a
sea shell path and curved it in among
it up slopes between boulder walls, and brought
it back upon itself, and she upon herself,
but could not put his face where they would know
he did it. He hid two, then stood up with the
one cleaned sheet and drew himself inside the
wordless block drawing two returning visions
he could not control, and they came and
worked on it, erasing him and his two dreams,
and left two dreams unnoticed under the cot.
When the cell was gotten ready for
the next one, the two dreams were put
in the trash by the attendant, who picked up
the last spot of dust with a wetted finger.
The dreams were burned with the trash,
and there are the ashes settling in the yard.
Cleanliness is next to godliness, they said.
The past and future are unclean when they
are spread out for inspection; when they
are erased, they are empty space, they are
the cleanliness of humans, but tempt
an unclean urge humans have to fill an
emptiness with lyric gods or demons,
which urge will not be cured until the last

15 The poet failed because he did not understand

dream is gotten out on paper and erased.
The poet failed because he did not understand   #15
he should have given us three empty
sheets marked new dreams for the old,
the infinitely subtle insight which annuls
in the very act of insight the nightmares
of both past and future, and sets three sheets
of paper free for multiple uses, for the poor,
say, to stuff in cracks in the plaster to keep
the shrieking wind quiet and winter warm,
or to stuff inside a coat and take edges
off the cold, or to wad inside a shoe.
The dream is a crucifixion on white paper.
The dream is a holocaust on white paper.
The dream is a resurrection on white paper.
The dream is an illumination on white paper.
The dream is a mad god on white paper.
The dream is forgiveness on white paper.
The dream is a poet on white paper.
White paper is not a dream when cleaned.
It may be set between two human beings.
When they agree to it, it is their godliness.

it was said: The embalmer found a poem
in the poet's mouth and concealed it for fear
he could not explain how it got there,
since every inch of life was under scrutiny.
He put it in his own mouth, and when
he loved his wife that night he tongued
the poem into her mouth and she knew fear,
and after love she never spoke a word or
it would come out with her speech
until she kissed her child to school and the
child grew stiff with fear when she felt
the wadded paper on her tongue and its
grassy taste of death. So she entered school
with a pallor no adult could miss,
and when called upon to tell who was
the Father of Humanity, her silence got her
taken to the washroom where she spat

16 Leave /Leave naked /Leave

the poem in the sink and her teacher turned
the color of the wall and slid the wad
of paper into a mark book and at the
close of school she smoothed it out
and put it with excuses, but panicked
and filed it with conduct, then thought
better and entered it with the diary
of the Father of Humanity, and when the
time to read that page arrived, she
could not skip that page for every inch
of life was under scrutiny, and so she read
Instructions To All Fathers of Humanity,
and said no name to it, so it was he who
said: Leave./Leave naked./Leave naked and   #16
hungry./Leave naked and hungry and lonely/
Leave naked and hungry and lonely and childless./
Leave./Leave boughs./Leave boughs and bushels./
Leave boughs and bushels and births/Leave
boughs and bushels and births and brethren./
Leave a tongue./Leave a larynx./Leave an ear./
Leave a sound./Leave it say./Leave earth its
Leave earth its gourd dirge/the shadows play
on the turning fields./Leave earth./Leave
a pucker on the earth's apple mouth./Goodbye./
As she read, they entered it in copy books,
and took it home to memorize, as with every
thought of the Father of Humanity, and every
parent hearing lessons was paralyzed with fear
and dared not show it, but with care explained
how truth must treat with enemies and
all their children, and treat with property
which must belong to government, and treat
with loyalty, and with the silence of submission,
and with corrupting sentiment as if it
were a sickened stomach from hard, green apples.
She heard their memory next day, and their
explanation, and the scrutiny of every inch
praised her for discovering what it knew was
not the Father of Humanity's, but took her
to great meetings where this fragment was
received as old but hidden authenticity,
and she explained this mystic summary of
all the Father of Humanity had taught
until one night she screamed goodbye!
goodbye! goodbye! over and over and over,
and they thought her ecstasy had come on

his last word, and she was at the purity of
leaving He had asked from total faithfulness,
so they took her clothes with awe, and
took her food with awe, and left her
in a space where no one went, and they kept
all seed from her with awe, and she wasted
to a tongue, a larnyx, and an ear, whispering
goodbye! as if there were a paper in her mouth.

he said: He picked up his cherished fiddle
after the holocaust and played a lament
for the jews, and a dirge for the gypsies.
Then he smashed his fiddle on the rubble
and said let music now lie down with them.
Then he went along the street called World
where he saw a dead sparrow, but his hands
were empty, so he sang in a cinder voice
a hymn for the sparrow: come back chirping, you
seeds ford the sparrow, grow it a tuft and a voice,
and flick it like a finger on whistling silk,
or a hand cleaning glass. Then he came
and he thought that was the image of curse,
the way the Jews and gypsies went, but his
hands were empty and he could not smash
music, so he looked back again and saw
the birds fly off in fear and the ass's
smell grow stronger, so he sang to the birds
the song the penitent sings at the foot of
a mountain where gods are white and cold:
"sin is rising to my nose, someone come and
take it, someone come and take my sin,
it lies along the road, it rises to my nose,
come and take it, make it white and cold!"
Then he saw a woman in a ditch stretched
out in rape, and white as alabaster,
and he smashed his empty hands down on
nothingness, and there was a silence like
eternity, so he buried her, and took out
one of his eyes and placed it over her head
and said watch the sky and when it comes
scream out she is here. Then the left side
of the world disappeared and he came on
spring crocuses where the earth is brown
water between banks of snow, and he

surged with delight at these golden angels
caught visiting the earth, but his hands were
empty, so he sang with a cinder voice: *"catch all*
spirits with gold and wind for a dance on
strings that rinse the ear with angel lore
or hands with the skin of an all night love."
Then he saw the woman he had buried in the ditch
run by him holding an eye in her palms,
and he thought to stop her for his eye,
but let her go, and looked at himself,
and saw his hand was a muted cello playing
a lullaby to the crocuses, and his other hand
was stroking out of a harp morning clouds,
and his one eye was a flute to a mad song
and every blade of grass was stone still with her
and he sat down and said I must come
to terms with this so the dead will be
grieved at my betrayal. So he cut off his
hand and plucked out his other eye and
went with a stick to the jews and gypsies
and placed both over them and said stay
until the sky comes and when it does scream
out here they are and point to the cinders.
Then with one hand and no eyes he left.
He went along the road called World with music
choking in his throat, but he heard screaming
and the sound of a fist beating on a door
so he said it is the sky, the sky has come to
find them. Or it is over again the killer come
to find them. No, it is the sky, the sky has come.
No, it is the killer, listen, the screams,
the thumps. But I left my hand and eye instructions
to scream and thump when the sky would come,
Then there was the great silence of eternity,
and he did not know which, and he went
back on his stick and one hand and felt
the ground and it was smooth with no traces.
Someone has come for them he said, the sky,
or some killer even of the dead. Then he
felt his hand begin to move as over the face
of a drum he could not see, soft rhythms,
in poplar trees, rhythms of waves on rocks,
and he began to sing in his cinder voice
for them who were taken by the sky or killers:
"the ocean is roaring while you are gone, roaring
and roaring at play: the rain is beating while

you are gone, beating and beating its way.
The leaves in the trees are clapping and leaping
while you are gone, the clouds are pursuing
the clouds, the clouds, while you are gone.
The woodpecker's heels have tambourine rings
in trees that are dead and hard from the sun,
and the hawks are screeching like strings
feeling frenzy of bows, while you are gone,
while you are gone the honey is dripping
from children's mouths, onto their golden skin,
women are running with eyes in their palms
to lovers who hide in cold mountains,
and sparrows fly in through a blind man's
sockets and sing to whistles of silk and
glass, clean is the wind! while you are gone."
Then he stopped. He knew that he had come
for them. He spent a long time seeking and found
his eye, then found his hand, but
the other eye was gone off to be a trumpet
with the woman. He found his cherished violin
and after years of repair he played again
a lament and a dirge for the ones he had found.

he said: He said I will know everything
the great God knows. I will love everything
the great God loves. God must not be alone
as everything and everyone arrives in God
for knowledge and for love. God will be moved
by anyone who wants this. So the God-knower
sat on a bench along skyscraper row and he knew
and loved everything that reached his senses.
At the end of the day, it was not enough, it
was not enough for him to go to everyone and
everything, they must come to him or
knowledge and love would fail. He returned to
the bench along skyscraper row with a sandwich
sign saying everyone come up to me so
I may know and love you as the great God
does. He passed the day giving out quarters
three or four times to the same bums who
had forgotten they had hit him up before.
At the end of the day, he could say nothing
to himself except the great God knows and loves
everyone and everything, and it must be this way

or the great God knows, loves nothing,
no one. So the God-knower said to himself
I will go up to God so God may know and
love me, then I will work out from what
happens who I should do as the great God
does. This is not folly I'm involved in,
the great God is present to everything and
everyone, so it is written. Someone who knows
and loves everything and everyone. So he sat
on the bench along skyscraper row and closed
his senses, though several times pickpockets
tried to steal from him, breaking his attention,
but he kept an inward silence and attention
worthy of a monk closed up in a wall.   An
image of every city and every person formed
on his mind, but they were all one city
and one person, then they faded into a cognition
that was not city, and no person, and he said
to himself, that is how the great God does it,
everything and everyone are a cognition which
is nothing and no one, so it must be a love
of nothing and no one.   How utterly simple!
At the moment I knew nothing and no one
I met the great God and the great God met me.
How utterly simple! Someone reached inside his
coat and he jumped awake and he heard
curses over someone's shoulder saying more
then shots were fired and he heard a woman
teller scream and he ducked below the bench
saying Jesus! that was close, and policemen
jumped behind his bench and opened fire
on fleeing robbers, and a child got caught in
the fire and fell and the getaway car smashed
sirens leaped against their chains, and the
action disappeared around a corner firing.
Then he said Jesus! that was close, but the child
is gone and maybe the woman teller. So he
cut out keeping his name to himself since
it would bring no one to life or to justice,
and he would only be able to babble what
he saw, and he was filled with a pity he
could not bear, and he walked avenues twitching
his head, trying to dislodge the pity he had
for the child, whom he saw as sleeping, sleeping
on a red patterned coverlet. He would wake up.
The woman teller who screamed would feed him.

He would play cops and robbers. Oh, God! No!
They would be shadows of buildings on buildings.
Sirens would be hysterical sopranos or
electronic masturbations or another innocence.
When his panic was over, then he met the great God.
He had missed his own vision. Everything
was this thing.   Everyone was this one.   That
is how the great God knows and loves. How
utterly simple, he said, but he was still sobbing
as if two weather fronts were meeting in him,
and he met the great God again. There are
many one things and many ones, who all
were at the robbery and killing; there are many
more one things and many ones who lead
up to the robbery and killing, and who will live
with it touching them He knew he had seen
every one thing and every one. But there was
no love in him. He had escaped into fantasy,
had loved the fantasy until it turned to cops
and robbers. So he stopped walking and stopped
twitching his head to clear it of its panic
and held still and let every detail of
what had happened rise up in his memory;

17 Everything is gone, of you, of me

then he nearly broke with love, it was not a
fantasy to see those bodies, that action, as if
they were not robbing and killing. It was
perversion of material to make of flesh and
sound and motion a curse on the goddam rich.
And the shadows of the building an escape route.
All the loveliness perverted into lethal panic.
Someone picked his pocket, someone spat on his shoe,
and the contradiction grew more fiercely inside
him of a love that expanded as lethal action
grew, or as he was ripped off by the ripped off.
Then he knew the burden of the great God. He turned
and went back. Without being noticed he stood
over the child's blood stain. He just stood.

IV REPROACH

I said: When we sit like this
everything is gone, of you, of me,   #17
of the world, except I sense you in
my head, my eyes in the shadow
at the back, you where the light would
come through, and I send snow flurries
across the transparent darkness into
I have no history, nor do you.
There is no feeling, there is restraint.
I have no urge to perform the tricks
of worthiness, nor any desire to hear
demands from you. The less
I know of your passion, the more I can
make you submit; the less you know
of mine, the more unflinchingly
you may command. That storm of
paranoia enters across between us
left to right and it is gone. And my
eyes remain watching and I know
you are where my eyes were,
where the light comes through. It is
as if I think talk or doing of love
is nowhere in the issues. One makes
poetry in the streets of May, one
makes justices in the trials of October.
In presences, one makes silence.
It is clear I am holding back your

love. Here is why. I would have
to open my skull and let
everything in it loose. My control
of you would go out in the sun
without dark glasses from pitch
dark to pitch light. So, I do it.
Gold double eagles. I'll tell you
what I see. So far still paradisal,
apricots now, some heads of new children
packed together, you could walk on them,
now their faces drooling innocence,
their eyes drooling blue, now her face,
it is not drooling, it is gold with blood
suffusing it, it is turning black,
inward on itself from looking at me,
a purple black, and it is turning away
in a curtsey style and leaving,
and the apricot space all around is
turning to follow her as into a navel
leaving me looking into a bell,
now the bell stops toward me,
its purpled bronze will not swing
down. This is what I have done to
innocence. It is like lantern weeds,
dead stalks with leaf lanterns in brown-
purple agitated by cold air. Then
it is my great wisdom to keep you
dark where my eyes were or you
will grow from gold to apricot to
infant to her face purpling into
a warning only killed innocence can
make stopped still in cold north air.
Or it is what has happened to innocence
looking at me. It has done nothing
to me and lost itself. You have done
something to me you did not explain
and you have lost yourself. If I
say I love you will that make it right?
Not until I know what I am that
empurples innocences. There you
are still in the place of my eyes.
You know I feel that I was innocent
that time when I curled from apricot
openness into the purple bronze bell
stuck on its upswing. It was like
the caving in of light flesh as if a

mother rolled half on you and it
became a consolation you never knew
was lethal until asleep half breathing
when dreams were left to do the
warning with means so indirect
you woke up crying from them not from
her but she woke and made it right,
but the depths of innocence were gone.
If this made me vengeful?
If this made me accusatory?
If this locked my skull at the top?
inside it no one show flesh?
No one be apricot, or in the sun?
Or are you telling me of your innocences?
There is no gold flesh to you after
so many loves! Was that time of me
a share of you, through cold reason
that said what way it was, and warm
feelings turned in upon themselves
and went into a navel quietude?
I think we are injured innocences.
We are like burn victims who love
through speech in the dark. I have
not felt I would speak to you from
innocence, with its apricot scars.
If I could, I could say I love you.
I could perhaps hear it from you.
The lights could come on inside my
skull and we could form a burn
victims anonymous to get help.

I said: All someone has to do
is strike the right note or put the right
color on paper and I think
it is revelation. You needn't say
a word to me.   It is as if you
are right here as guarantee.
It is contrived, but so what, what
is contrived is a perfect note or color.
When a face is the right note or color,
the revelation is a rinse of me.
When it is a face free of coercion or
cooption, one I see reading a book,
or watching a sales pitch,

I have no trouble with infinities,
with unending love, with realms
of being that discard ideas
as used shotgun cartridges which
artists make into the beard
on a war god mask. I am in awe
when a face is right. When
it speaks and the speech is right,
I have no defense. If the speech
is to me and it is right,
I have no gravity. The uplift is
a miracle. I am helpless.
It is the best state in the world.
I could be under a pile of rocks.
You know the words I mean,
the right name, the real name
for someone, nothing laid on,
nothing ripped off, that moment
which must be infinite when
the real name for someone is said,
for something. It is revelation,
the right note, or color.
Love grows from there.
It is unstoppable. Maybe I live
with small names, so have
felt some unstoppables. But when
someone says your name, and
the name is right, a wonderful set
of mountains, a sky, a sea,
and a crowd fill space.

18 I want you to do what you do

When someone says your name and
it is wrong, the circus tent
collapses on a pitiful crowd, who
escape, no harm, but are sick
with fear, I do not want you
to name yourself. Balcony stuff.
I want you to do what you do   #18
so we can say the right name,
the dimple in the water an oar
pulls, a slam bang fight,
a lie talced and slid into a shoe,
a vow that is browned chicken
eaten late at night,
as if the metaphors were grunions
and took their risks with tide
and sand to put some undetected
life between the flashing ankles
of fisher boys and fisher girls.
When I say your name and
it is right, I am a bowl
of joy of light. When it is wrong,
I am drying in corn stalks
and my love is gone. You know
I have spent nights in winter
fields. You know you have
held me up to the light. I set
hold the cobs of indian corn.

She said: You, never had to seduce me,
nor I you. You thought so. You thought
you could yield to those autumn mornings
permissibly so long as I had no breasts,
to those blue evenings so long as I
had no thighs. Blake's angel, or
sexless Wisdom lovely in blue. I
could permissibly be lured to
console you. I wanted only to show
you that I could love and what,
and was not some conditioned reflex
working mechanically on glands.

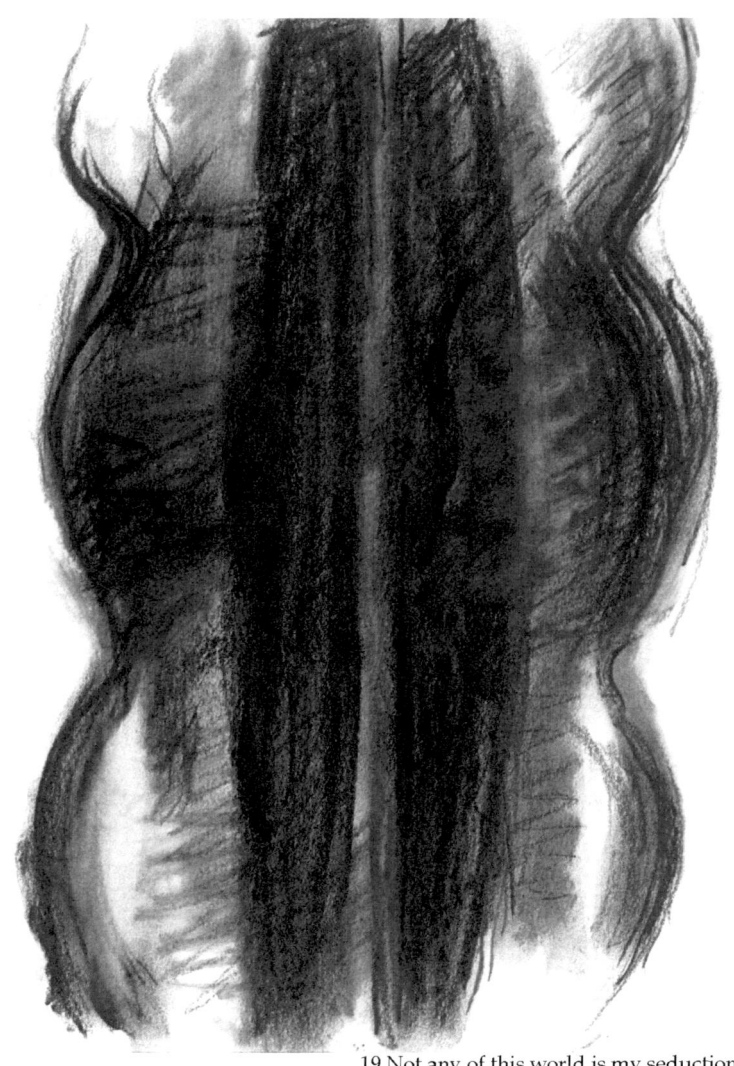

19 Not any of this world is my seduction

Not any of this world is my seduction,   #19
not any of it is yours. I loved you
because you were like something
poured, not out of a ladle, out
of the pot. And there was no emptiness.
There were thumps of potato to you,
yes, the spitting of exposed wires,
yes, but always an instinct to pour,
something to fill lungs or grass yards.
I saw you come to emptiness.
I saw you baffled, humiliated.
I would not come for lure of
pity, it was a grief for me not to;
I would not come for the lure of
shambles, nor for the pounding of
the empty pot. You had to know
your pouring out was your doing.
You had to come back to your own
doing, no one else's pouring out
could substitute. You could not
be a ventriloquist's dummy.
You are pouring out again. It is
not anyone else. Yet it is everyone.
Gatherings of the senses,
smeared across autumn sundowns,
the chimney swifts drunk with smells.
We have been since to crematoria.
Twist upwards in a throat like the heart
starts up many times. I will
tell you again I love what pours
out of itself, I always have,
not human venom, you know this,
but the clarities or the darknesses
that are livid self pouring.
I cannot hold either in my hands.
I have put my hands under them
and been blessed. There is a mystery
the expanse of the sea to the moment
someone gives that way. There is an
anxiety the length of the sky to watch
where. There is a wait like hell's
to watch someone go through emptiness.
Heaven is fullness pouring itself out.

V REPAIR

They must paint the god
each time with sand the same
or home for the dead.
The dance with the mask must be.
The cyclamen start as questions.
They finish too close to the sun, falling
head before wings to a loam sea,
the fall into isolation.
The snow outside a window is
a cycle gang to, go escort only so far,
then the solo into isolation,
the same each time.
Think of who goes away, what,
the nests for cocooning a re-entry,
the edges of spring marked
do not cross yet, but the love
that is handed in with IDs,
handing always the same,
same stamp, same storage, chit,
no one there, can be no one,
no sense to someone,
a dancing bear, a flying serpent,
a thunderbird, a trinity, a one,
a void teeming with void,
it is the trick of dry ice in hot water,
the ghost out of the ground as
a worm from too much rain,
the same whom colors summon
to squares and half moons of sand
the it of the time of the spring solstice,
the it of the no sense, or of time
discovered lagging on itself, or crystals not
matching when the sword breaks on
a hard bone, the chance, who
says the chance at the minute of
going of permanence, a laugh
leaping out on the other side of a
dead throat, unassailable now, in
one's own hands, not a new skin
for a wall, for someone's trap door,
the ear hears the regular beat,
hears the bubbles of soap break,
hears the language so tired it goes
off its spool high speed like tapes,

the mask realizing no one is in it,
no one comes to it, holds its
through, does not move, forgets
which god must come, that
isolation which is the coal miners come
up without the trapped and those
at the pithead were forewarned,
and there is silence and only eyes
to let in light, to let out nothing,
isolation away from one's own times
or mistake, as they are exhibits
marked out of reach and admitted
as evidence in the self and nowhere
they are not there, their images are
gagged by bench ruling, they are not
to be tampered with, they are
the same each time each trial session.

After irradiation,
run to the flattest spot of the blast
at point zero, draw a circle
there, call it the sun, and stand on it
until the sun dies, then make
an S in the circle for the moon, stand
on it until the moon dies,
erase the S and put in a cross, lie
down on it like a savior,
then rise up and scratch out the circle
with your toe then run back
and lie on your cross until the wind dies,
as it will soon, then dig twelve deep
holes inside the smudged circle
and shout so you vibrate
the sky and stars will fall like fruit
into the holes, and you must
fill in each one as fast as they fall,
then go back and stamp the dirt
down firmly, then make a low moan
and she will come out of darkness
looking with sympathy for
the victim who moans and you must
not let on you are only irradiated
until she forces it from your lips,
then she will be stunned,

and she will go off into the night
knowing she may not hand this on,
and she will not ever be seen,
then you are to applaud, as if you had
the world's one game going,
and he will come and you may
grin at him immediately
and tell him so he will think
perhaps he was not close enough to the
bomb to be contaminated,
so he will run in her direction,
catching her scent, knowing this proof
of his cleanliness was out ahead,
then you must dance wildly, but be careful
not to get exhausted for the night is long,
and crickets will come and cicadas
and brighten sillily your hoarse bass self
accompaniment, and in a short time
they will rub marshmallow limbs,
be depressed and fall, but ducks will rise
up at night and clothesline themselves,
then heat will begin to flake and
descend on your head as petals from a
shaken dogwood, then the cold will begin
to snap sticks, snap rocks, snap itself
and gravel will, pile up at your feet;
you must stop dancing then. You must   #20
reach up to the black sky and rip sheets

20 You must reach up to the black sky

of it off and stuff them under the pile
you made of the splinters, then you
must re-draw the circle around point
zero, quickly, because the flash of the
day's bomb has nearly made it
around curved space, its white ring
of heat approaches at an infinite speed,
then you must stand on top of the kindling,
and when the heat flash hits white
there will be one flesh colored burst of
flame dyed into the white firing
ring as it goes through making it a
defiant rainbow, you being it,
sprayed through it like wild paint
and you will go with it forever round
and round in rainbow exultation.

she said: A woman comes to you.
You do not know her. She strips and says
lay me. You have many counselors.
One says you may only love her.
You say I may only love you, who are you?
She dresses and walks away from you.
Then she comes back with her album and says
here is my first poem, about pussy willows.
When I was seven they were soft on hard
when everyone was hard, they were earliest soft,
and left me, not for their own fault.
My second poem has to do with breasts
and the changed look in my father's eyes.
I call breasts angels I seduced and
they shamed me by forcing their way out.
The more delightedly I imprisoned them,
the more they shamed me.
My third poem is a pure abstraction.
It is a human geometry: family, male,
female, as cones, triangles, tangents,
and relationship is marked in alchemically.
The rest of the poems spin off from this.
The hard is never soft, the soft

21 Open senses are a crucifix

never hard. I bring images to thoughts.
It is a matter of those cardboard designs
used to measure intelligence time,
and I always have an unfitted piece.
Laying is a thought that says peaches.
but means stainless steel sphere.
I know this, but try it again and again.
Then the woman closes the album.
She gets up to go and says you may
love this. You have many counselors.
One says you must know more than this.
You say it. She says I am all day
filled with emotions of flesh and form.
I want no satisfaction. It is
this double image, not a matter of optics,
sometimes delight, mostly ravishment.
I have a friend with clear face and freckles.
I see brown stars falling out of her flesh sky.
I love her for it and she has a corner curled smile.
But I see someone shaking a juke box,
furious at it for playing the wrong rock 'n' roll.
I see triage. I see the good of the species
the calculus of abortion. I've seen those
eerie homunculi, like the pet crocs
people flush down the drains and they live with
flashlight eyes in sewers. Laying is a
cleared space in all this. It is flesh on
flesh without the cutlery rattling of
property, eternality, quenching of fires;
it may be the last innocence. Love this.
Then she walks away. You have many
counselors. One says let her go
if you are to love her. You let her go.
She comes back later and says I found
this keen poem, it says open senses   #21
are a crucifix, a holocaust, the soul
is a sunburned thing, it has a metal box
begging coins it rattles for the poor,
the hard and the soft are one.
She gets up and hurries away. You have
one counselor who says let her go.
She comes back soon with a slashed painting
and says this is a rape.
I want you to see what it really is.
This is the double image. What is the last
innocence? You have one counselor

who does not know. So you say,
read me the keen poem. She reads,
the soul is a sunburned thing.

he said: He came to the rock of questions
and he sat down. There was the rock of answers
but no one came to it. He thought no one
comes because I have not asked, so he said,
how do I get back my soul? No answer.
The rock of answers reddened, so he said,
how do I get back my body. No answer.
The rock paled. These were mortal questions
left without response. He got up and crossed
to the rock of answers where he sat down
and said, you get your soul back when you
wake up. You get your body back too.
He giggled then to have squirmed out of his
two questions. You get your soul back
when every mouth is fed. You get your body
back when every bullet is spent.
He choked on these two answers and looked
down symbolizing the weight of that knowledge.
Someone came and sat on the rock of
questions and he heard her whisper, please,
how do I get my soul back? He said, you
get your soul back when you wake up.
Honest, lady, that's the way it happens,
and you get your body back too!
I could tell you something else, but that would
curve your spine. There was a silence
silent as depression, sunlight going west.
You get your soul back by giving up lies
the silence intensified. She waited as
space waits. You get your soul back, he said,
by rummaging through a bin until you find it,
then you pay for it and it's yours.
You get your soul back by crying when
You should or laughing when you should.
You get your soul back when you tell
the truth if it, costs you an arm to your elbow.
The silence was now brutal. She was waiting
for what had not come. He said,

You get your soul back if I give it to you,
Here. There was emptiness between them.
She took it and said, how do I get back
my body? The same way, he said. Here.
She took the emptiness between them.
She filled with joy. She rose and left him
seated on the rock of answers. He said,
what happened there? and he went back
quickly to the rock of questions and sat
again to wait, and she came and sat
on the rock of answers with this smile
on her face that was the soul of blue.
She arranged her garments so one shoulder
showed and she swept her hands
between them unrolling a bolt of
emptiness, smoothed the bolt and said
ask me whatever you wish. He said,
you are mocking my futility. Those
questions are precious to me. Even
my stupid answers show you this.
I have your soul and body to give back
to you, she said. Here. If you want them.
No, he said, they look better on you.
Besides you are on the rock of answers.
It's a place I'd rather not be. Then
you must ask whatever you wish,
she said. Is there peace in the body
ever while it has itself back, he said,
while what happens lunges through it?
Is there peace in the soul, or does it
interrogate the body with blinding lights?
No, she said, neither asleep or awake.
But when you lay one soul upon another
and the two are without lies,
there is a kind of peace, a fervent
kind, though nothing of what happens ceases.
Sometimes the same is true of bodies.
Now you sit here and you tell me, she said.
There is a time of peace, he said, but it
is fearful, it is a stance of truth, like
a shedding of both soul and body.
It can't be like that, she said. Right,
he said, but that's the only way to say it.
Let me sit there, she said, and try again.
There is peace in the soul and in the body,
she said, when they have themselves to give

no matter what they've been through,
or what will happen to them. That,
he said, would take care of the fierce
self hold we have. But what about the
rip off when we give, peace is a
shambles. You sit here, he said, and let
me try. Peace in soul and body comes
when you have both to give to someone
who gives them back, no, to someone
who gives you their's back. But that's
selfishness really, she said. Then,
it is your giving purely altruistically,
he said. But that's suicide, she said.
No, he said. There's a trick here.
No one will take them, so you have them
and you'll have peace because you
gave them away altruistically. I'll
take them, she said. If fact I've already
got them, both, from you.
That should frighten me, he said, but
it doesn't. It frightens me, she said,
but I will live with the fright. You
sit here, she said, and I'll give you mine,
and see if you sense the fright I mean.
I feel something, he said, not fear.
It's like lifting a jellyfish out of the water
with your bare hands. She said, thanks.
I only mean you can't do it, he said.
You've missed it she said, it's given.
 Now do you feel the fright. Yes, he said.
I wouldn't want to be god. God
would be awful fear. God is awful
fear, she said, from the rock of answers.
Like being a ceiling for bats mostly,
only with veins and lots of blood.
Bats are not vampires, he said, you've
got your imagination tangled up in this,
and that blows your answers. Back
here with you, the rock of questions.
Is god awful fear, she said. Yes,
he said. How is god awful fear, she said.
God doesn't come back to body or soul.
God hasn't got a body or a soul.
We're beyond that, she said, we're talking
about being given them by someone and so
getting them back and that's a fearsome

64

thing, god's got every body and soul
around, like getting food or bullets.
Get off that rock and I'll tell you.
God is something that was given away
completely in the beginning. Except there was
this fully lonely spot god could feel.
Then the bits and, pieces started coming
back, given into that lonely spot,
hell souls, heaven souls, or something
like that, hell bodies, heaven bodies.
So the lonely spot get filled with terrific
fear about how to handle the pieces,
because it's god coming back to god,
and what contradictions and betweens!
So, god's got to put god together again,
and god looks like a madman's mosaic,
Wait, he said, how do you know stuff
like this? She said, well look at it, stupid,
how else can it be, you didn't pull
yourself out of your own throat like
reversing a sock. You asked the questions.
God is not the sum of us, he said.
I didn`t say god was, she said. I said
god gave everything away and was
a lonely spot waiting to see if anything
came back. A mixed bag came back.
So god is not a blue bolt of emptiness.
You stay there and I'll ask, he said, because
I think god is not a spot of loneliness,
God is like slave ground which grows
everything and has no choice but doing it
like air you can do anything with,
so god is not lonely, god is livid pain
or livid joy with everyone laying it on.
Sounds insensate, really, she said. No,
but you're right, he said, god gave it all
away in the beginning, but I say
god got caught in the mesh of the giving,
and is no lonely spot somewhere else
All right, ask, she said. Would you
give your soul and body to god?
Yes, she said. Would you get creamed
if you did it? Yes, she said. Would god
when you gave yours to god? No, she said.
What do you mean, he said, that's
murder? No, she said, it's company

But I'd get creamed with you and
this god! Yes, she said, that's company.

he said: A tree said do you love me,
and I said, I guess so, and it withered
and started to die, so I said, yes, yes,
and it greened again and played jacks
with the heat waves. I knew I was caught
then. A mountain came up and asked me
the same and I guessed it was ready to
erode, ready to send rocks down on the
shrubbery, into the silver stream to choke it.
I said, yes, I love you, and it returned
to its rank and the word spread with the snow.
I have now no nuances to live with.
I mean a life of my own feelings,
if I prefer one day to look down from a ledge
on lace surf on a shallow beach
and delight in the large, smooth, hiding
rocks at surf's edge and their converse
when the undertow is just right, as if
a door opened and closed quickly on an
audience of bass voices all talking.
As if the cormorants zip back and forth
wanting their full share, and the rust in
the folds of the blue water under the lifting
fog as the sun mixes its paints through it,
or the cliffs usually blinded into dunness,
now out with delicate rusts and yellows.
If they only knew it was not choice I made
when I enjoyed the jockey club rocks,
but choice I made when each came with
their opposite selves as a threat and said,
do you love me, and I said, yes, yes,
to keep disaster away. I have seen such
bitten fingers. I have seen faces lashed from
inside, as if the surface veins were proof,
though they are not. The passions of justification.
It's not gently any more, these comings,
these raging justices saying do you love me
and I say, yes, yes, or raging injustices
will make a havoc in a roomful of porcelains.
They don't mean love, though I do!

I say love and they hear fire! shoot! rub out!
They hear obey! submit! root out! pluck out!
They hear horrible things. As if from my lips!
Though some hear the sea make lace and the rocks
approve with bass voices when a door quick opens

There was a blue-black desert with hills   #22
to it and no end over which a black rag hawk
flew in circles, and I knew there was a life
there, it was edible, and the hawk was hungry.
Along the road were truly orange flowers
small and making it despite the wind.
As the sea, the desert was the parable.
My senses are flooded with the hidden issues.
I know that hawk, I know that wind
right out of the sun, its thirst, the tongues
it leaves twisted up in the dust of a wash.
As I know those smooth loaf rocks of slate.

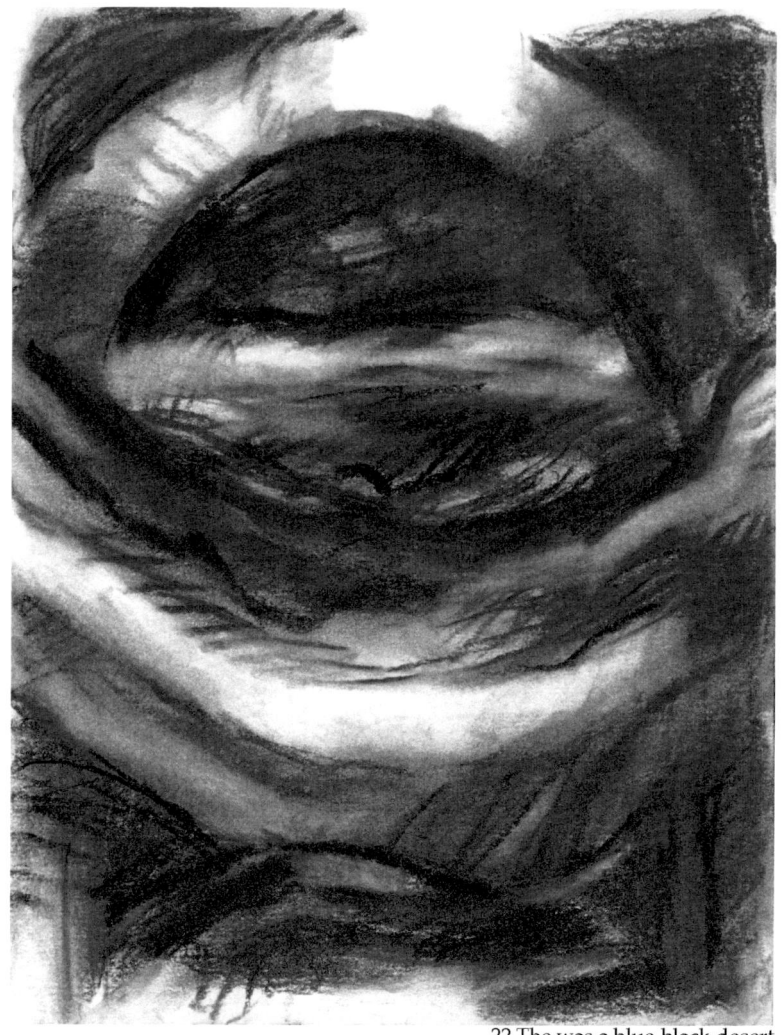

22 The was a blue-black desert

I love it all, yes, yes; it is no license.
Arid the white moon staring at me for answers,
and the star it has on a leash barking
at me for approaching, and the trees that
must dream the days in uneasiness and sleep-
talk no one records, so the dreams recur.
There is a red berry thick thorn bush crowded
with snails in their shells in autumn.
They feed so slowly they die, between bites,
dozens of them, and as I watch them everything
slows down to a century's caress, a century's
feelings, loving, moving, an aeon's precarious
shell swaying through the thickest hindrances.
It's a delight! It's a laugh! They are serious!
They must lug their own beauty.

23 When the tongues spoke

VI RECALL

she said: He learned it all
when the first tongue said, those are my
olives, my soil, that is my wall,
when the second tongue said,
that is my wheat to the mountain's rise.
He learned it all
when the third tongue said my women,
and the fourth tongue said my men,
and the fifth tongue said my cattle,
my barn, my dung, my thresher ox,
he learned it all.
And he was young when the tongues spoke, #23
he was young when war went sowing,
still young when it bore a harvest in,
when it peeled souls like bark off twigs
and made of them baskets of hatred.
He learned it all
when the first one saw the moon disrobe,
when the second one saw the moon lie down,
when the third one saw no one come,
when the fourth one knew and sang a dirge,
when the first one saw the moon get up,
and dress and take a basket to the fields,
and cut white grapes and press clear wine,
and fill a cup and drink it dry as glass.
And he was young
when the first one said a shepherd's sky,
and the second one said a king's,
and the third one said a scapegoat sky,
and the fourth one said a potter's.
He learned it all
when the first man sat like a withered tree,
and the first woman sat like a parchment scroll,
and the second man sat like a vat of oil,
and the second woman sat like a wick lamp lit.
And he was young
when he touched her skin,
when he stacked bricks up for a wall,
when he straightened the trees,
when he pitted and cured the olive yield:
He learned it all

when he answered the curse,
when he answered the killing,
when he answered the coins,
when he answered the judgment.
And he was young
when they made him a tree.
And he was young
when they made him its fruit.
And he was young
when they made him a grave.
And he learned it all.
And he was young
when the wheat went out to the mountain's rise,
and the moon took its glass of dry, white wine,
and the women could kiss far off with their eyes,
and the men could sing where the withered tree rose.

I said to her he was intensity itself,
yet a calmness, so I said, that's presence,
nothing like it! She said to me he learned
it , the glow of stained glass if you are
the light and you come to him, he has
worked through the colors and the leadings,
you are the glow he has. It is not as in
flesh then, I said to her. Yes it is, she said
to me, you must watch bodies closely,
they reflect you if you love them
and they can take loving as he can after
he broke the patterns of disturbance.
Do you cling to the image as to money?
I want to cling to the body, I said
to her. That's why his presence meant
intensity to me, not to cling to him,
but to myself, that way, as he,
but that's where the dark spot always
sits in my center and knows itself
as its own genetic code, out of my reach,
at least I think, and I go away,
as now, and cannot sit in myself,
there is not room. She said to me,
there is a passion to him. The clarity
came from a passion. Every day, every
night has been to that glass.
I have sat days when the slate sun

drained his life blood, when the cold
sun broke in icicles off his design,
and when the nights were a living death.
There were days of the torrent of light
and nights of soft luminosity. Often
I would be entranced watching
the whole of his ablaze, if blues and
greens blaze, or I would be without end
in the empty, lifeless glass. I would
close my eyes then and let him go.
I know what it is to be the dark center
of a self. It's the way of knowing nothing
must be. He has been a dark center.
I said to her, is it flesh or glass he is?
She said to me, am I flesh telling you
the way love glows in him or anyone,
if it were pitch dark and our voices
were the only real difference from night
and I told you I was illumined by
your love would you say she's glass?
And if I had no body would I not
be flesh if I said I love you intensely?
Forgive this. It is unintended schooling.
It is true for me when his love glows
unspoken, even when it is gagged by
darkness, it is flesh, if he has none,

24 If you love someone

if he has none ever, it is flesh, it
glows as flesh with love, it dullens
as flesh with hate, it goes out with hatred.
He is always that way, I said to her.
He is, she said to me. I'm stunned,
I said to her. How is it possible he does
not blow up, or melt, whatever the metaphor?
She said to me, if you love someone   #24
who becomes as your soul you have two strengths.
One is you may risk everything of yourself
at every moment because you can be
recreated at every moment. One is you may
risk everything of everyone else at every
moment because you can recreate it.
You know what it is. Do you do that for him,
 I said to her. That is what I do, she said
to me. Then you have a greater passion, I
said to her. I know the dark center, she said.

he said: they found the first body smiling
over a mug of coffee in an all night beanery.
The counterman noticed. They found no marks,
just the smile, but no Buddha sort,
more outward as if he saw through closed eyes.
The second body showed up in an auto graveyard,
behind the wheel of a wrecked Jag, dead still
with pure joy: it saw everything through lids.
They were swinging the magnet over the Jag
when the crane man spotted this quiet flesh.
Not a mark, not a thing wrong,
dead from joy, as if dead from pure oxygen.
They checked out the third body in a cat house,
again, beatific smile, no foul play,
a livid joy as if seeing the world through
a mask. They had to discount the two children
found in the library by the cleaners late behind
the globe in the reference section, the globe
still spinning as if they had hypnotized
themselves to death. There was probably cause
there, not the mystery of the others.
But their intense happiness set fear loose
in a way the other deaths had not.
Then there were no more deaths, but people were

75

found wandering the streets by patrolmen
not stoned, not bombed, not sexed up,
but so happy they could scarcely walk upright
men and women, though no young people.
They were sobered up, and tested, but each time
the question touched the one area,
they would fill with joy that made them shake,
so the questioners had to back off.
Several priests went on TV and explained it
was the beatific vision a divine vision no
human could take in the body. Such was the beauty
of it, some had died and some were maimed.
God had forgotten mystery and had been seen,
causing such intense joy they had died or flaked.
Or god had done it purposely, indiscriminately,
and was likely to do it again. Dark glasses
sold by the millions, though the priests said the
vision was inward, in pure spirit, which was why
the joy seemed to see right through closed lids.
No one looked up, anything beautiful was covered.
There was an anger at these violations,
at someone who killed with intense happiness.
It was like, but only like, radicals who blew
themselves up because of a dream of purity,
the dream the killer of inexpert dynamiters.
Out with that one! But several druids on TV
said no, it was the vision of the marrow hope
of man that welled up suddenly as lake mist in
them who died or flaked, as if under the waters
of the mind the fairy world sang ecstasies the
usual wind of the world kept troubled and down,
but in some stillness of the victims the full
music killed them with unbearable loveliness,
and everyone walking in the wind of the world
had best not be still or the music would rise
and there would be deaths beyond counting, or a
city full of loose low clouds colliding, colliding.
Horoscopists kept pointing to regions of the sky
saying, power came from there accidentally
into unready structures and blew their fuses.

The police files were all marked unsolved and
stored, but a wisdom committee sat and said,
it is the fairies and the music of the marrow
of hope which, if loose in the human frame,
destroys it or renders it foolish.

Let everyone walk in the wind of the world.
Then the druids got on TV and said,
they are shrewd, the fairies and their music,
and rogues who wear practical clothes.
You hear them sing when you pass them, or think
you think about your-power or budgets or fees,
their music is so disguised you do not hear it
and you are likely to die or to flake
from what you think is no music but practical
cloth, so you must partly listen,
though it is dangerous, and know when they trick
you toward joy or sorrow in practical clothes.
That way you'll keep life in your fist and not
open your hand to explain. The wisdom
committee got afraid that the druids had taken
precaution away, the wind of the world
solution. They reconvened and struck out
of their counsel the fairies and wind
and said, too much joy or sorrow destroys life,
each one must have a personal gauge.
Indices of general joy and general sorrow are
to be found posted in government locales.
They the found someone walking naked
on a main drag and his body glowed with
the suspect joy, but he made perfect sense
when they caught him, fully self-possessed
and when they tried to clothe him,
the clothes evaporated, and he was human,
and spoke every known tongue, and was
at home with food, and could not be contained,
and was not violent, and raised no lust.
He said: to die from too much joy is choice;
to be stunned by it, a choice, as with sorrow.
They said, you are not human with such choice.
Then his glow swallowed itself and he was shamed.
So they clothed him. And they closed his file.
But they found him wandering next day,
scarcely able to walk upright, not stoned,
not bombed, not sexed, the happiness trip.
The day after they found him dead smiling
out through closed lids at the world.
They said, we did it when we said
it was not human to have such choice.
The priests went on TV and said no. He
said they didn't have to die for joy,
or for sorrow. It was that they couldn't

give up the joy to live the human scene.
Only beatific vision in life causes death.
He died of beatific vision. It's the fairies,
said the druids on TV. Improper precautions,
he did not know his gauge, he let in
excessive amounts, judged the wisdom group.
We did it with the stuff about choice,
they said again, he swallowed the joy
to hide it when we said not human,
put it in the file; operating procedure--
do not tell a glowing naked man he
is not human, nor glowing naked woman,
nor child. They will swallow what
is visible and it will kill or craze them.
It's the fairies, said the druids on TV.
They open up a hole in you and you fall
down into their music. No, they said,
look at the dead, they come right through
their lids at you, and the walking ones rain on you.
It's not anyone's glow but theirs.
It's beatific vision, said the priests on TV.
It overflows the soul and kills the body.
Bullshit, they said, the victims knew
they could not blame possession. Even
dead, they saw the world through joy.
That's why these gauges are crucial. You
must know if bees feeding on chrysanthemums
in your eyes are too much. If waves hurling up
flak at gulls from rocks are too much like war,
if the blood of the dead is too much like corduroy,
if the lies floating like pelicans for fish are
charming, sailing, garbage bags. The charms that
are not charms, the not charms that are charms.

25 He stood up and bats came

It's the fairies, said the druids on TV. Themselves.
You must know if the faces puncture your nerves.
You must know what you can take, it's in
each thing, each one, held down, let loose.
It's the beatific vision, said the priests on TV.
No, it's the fairies, said the druids, and they
hanged, "the lyre of the trees and fingers
of rain and songs for the wind is the fairy's
way, and drowned is the way of man in them!"
They said, you must know the words that get
filled taut, those that can explode joy or
sorrow on you They may differ even day to day.
There may be the one touch of the whole world
out of a child's voice and tapestries without
weight might just float down on your head.
You must suspect every one thing every one
minute, for a star, to a snail shell, to
a kiss, or to a curse, or a rocket, or a gun.
Accept choice as standard operating procedure.

I said:
He stood up and bats came.   #25
He stood up and doves came.
It was the same he
who sat down and blood flowed,
who sat down and skin healed.
It was the same he
who walked and fruit dried,
who walked and buds grew.
It was the same he
and sunstorms flared
when he talked,
and moonstorms cured,
and raged held whetstones
when he talked,
and love held chamois rags.
 It was the same he,
and there were splitting logs
when he talked,
and there was tearing cloth,

26 When you are not mine

and there were gavels falling.
It was the same he,
and there was nailing up,
and there was gassing down,
and there was frying
when he talked,
who sat down and lyrics came,
who sat down and drizzle came,
who sat down and sprouts came.
It was the same he
who drew each one a rorschach blot,
and put two cells in a fertile dish,

and set three wheats in a single field,
and tied four winds to spinning light.
It was the same he
who stood up, and bats and doves.

I said:
When you are not mine,   #26
and I am not yours,
there are swallows out for us
in a sky that covers their tracks.
When you are not mine,
stories are roadside pumpkin stacks
and my mouth waters,
and cider holds to its sandy gallons.
When I am not yours,
seeds sit in your hand like small
birds your dog noses after,
who cannot see the wind take them.
You have that desert.
I have this air cleared of dust.
I can see rivets on the bridge
miles away, a fog
held like a herd of cattle out
ttouches of feeling,
touches of colored brushes
on glass and luminous minutes.
You tasting the screech
in the water, the flail in the bread,
watching a woman weep,
watching a man dung a tree,

the smooth flanks of a mountain,
salt with a finger,
oil and strokes of hair,
who throw rocks.
When I am not yours
I live with fumes, drink
carcinogens, have no swallows
but cars, and I am the space
that dodges, or must not breathe
or drink. But the faces!
Each a one, an instant, gone,
then one. Kinds without duplicate.
 When you are not mine
the mountain is quiet, its angels
off scouting, the olive trees
even at night resist the sun
with fierce muscles, and visions
come whose teeth
leave no marks, or whose balm
is odorless. You own them.
Your jeopardy.
When I am not yours
I love the storm centers of wood,
and wide eyes,
and hands that need no voice,
and the woman who cut
flowers from the air
and left them on children's pillows.
When you are not mine,
you love lilies and sparrows
and white stone
defying the blinding sun,
and clean straight bodies
leaping flagstones in a dance.
When you are not mine,
and I am not yours,
words are out for us flying
breakneck through orange trees

27 I thought time and sun would crack

after mates and challengers.
Their chatter plucks our fruit.

she said
I thought time and sun   #27
would crack the varnish of these sills.
Memory built of events when
his voice made up spirits for places he
crossed, but they did not.
Love leaves traces
without there being a mark, you
knew those mountains were wolf tooth
to someone who stood on this rock
and looked west just after the sun and
there was its ripped flesh,
or someone's horse shied at the ferocity
in the slavering color of rays.
His love was here.
It is a ruined place.
He said he loved the awkward stones.
He left the widow spirit
who does not grieve but stays and
knows the history of this place.
The spirits of the bones
are the most awesome of the widows.
They keep fierce secrets.
They keep fierce hopes.
They keep their words like wells
screeching for each pail.
Words have been laid on these places,
bells on the necks of goats,
always the slight noise somewhere,
all day and all night,
as if the air were hit with light taps
while nothing visible moved.
Love is a trace.
Even in wildernesses.
Someone has seen the laughing rocks.
Someone has seen them weeping.

he said:
He had her face before him.

She was reading stock reports aloud.
He looked away for a moth.
She was reading a recipe for gumbo aloud.
He looked away for a lotus Ford.
She was reading children's grades aloud.
He looked away for hip-huggers.
She was reading Jeremiah's Lamentations aloud.
He looked away for maple seed spinners.
She was reading Gray's Anatomy aloud.
He looked away for Phantom jets.
She was reading Holy Living and Holy Dying.
He looked away for checkered vests.
She was reading mail order catalogues aloud.
She was reading the urban Yellow Pages.
She was reading Social Registers aloud.
He looked away for a pulsar watch.
She was reading Joy of Sex, More Joy of Sex,
she was reading Massage Techniques aloud.
He was looking away for hockey scores.
He looked away for limericks.
He looked away for wine lists.
She was reading wine lists aloud.
He had her face before him.
He looked away for Magellanic clouds.
Her face was gone before him.
She was reading Bears to him aloud.
He looked away for alternating hips.
He looked away for snarling downward gears.
He looked away for jockeys and for weights.
Her face was gone before him.
He was reading Paradise Regained aloud.
He was reading Kafka's Metamorphoses.
He was reading Endings of the World.
Her face was gone before him.
He turned away to bourbon and branch.
He turned away to scotch and water.
She was reading comic strips in silence.
He had her face before him.
He was reading UFO's in silence.
She had his face before her.
They were reading scandal sheets in silence.
His face was gone before her.
She was reading Madams' diaries.
She was reading mystics' levitations.
She was reading metaphors of raping.
His face was gone before her.

She turned away for chilled tequila.
She turned away for cold duck.
She turned away for Irish neat.
He was reading Rake's Progress.
She was reading The Flying Dutchman.
He was reading Younger Frankenstein.
She was reading old Valachi papers.
She was reading Bears to him aloud.
They were before their faces.
He was reading her Quetzalcoatl.
She was reading him her mantra.
He was reading her advice.
She was reading him advice.
They were aloud before their faces.
She turned away for Triple Sec.
She examined center foldouts silently.
He examined center foldouts silently.
She was reading games that people play.
He was reading headship of St. Paul.
She was reading Virgil on the Amazons.
They were gone before their faces.

He said:
It has to be real.
She can't bag your soul.
Heat it in a spoon.
Close the shades to noon.
Shoot you in her arm.
It has to be real.
Tatooing on your body.
It won't come to harm.
This needle lays on blue.
Tatooing on a lady.
She will make you warm.
Shooting in your arm.
Who will make you you.
It has to be real.
You can't bag her soul.
It will leave you soon.
Like the shades of noon.
Like the colored lights.
All the frisbee lights.
They will leave you soon.
Empty of your soul.

Scooped out ice cream soul.
Garbage baggy soul.
She has to be real.
Can't make love a steal.
Steal a soul to feel.
It has to be real.
Lips to glue for real.
Hips to glue for real.
Soul to fix on soul.
Horses cannot pull.
It has to be real.
Or your heart is steel.
Heart is razor steel.

he said:
"God made your arm, man,"
Man threw it in with brushwood.
"God made your head, man.
Man threw it with cabbages.
"God made you all, man."
Man tossed it with trash
and stood burning, naked, white
gas flame on a wastage spout,
 God made the fuel, man."
Man turned off the gas,
and there was a fierce silence.
Into that one spot not man,
God put a question on a splint,
passed it through the spot
not man and it incinerated.
God put an answer on a sled
and opened the doors on the spot
not man and shoved it in,
and the answer volatilized.
God got on a toboggan and rode
into that one spot not man
and God was a quick breath
on glass then God disappeared.
Then out from the one spot no
man a rain came and stood,
a scepter was given into its hands,
then it was driven off by itself.
Then a piercing sun stood out.
Then a stone drunk moon,

and they were driven off together.
Then a searing wind stood out,
was spun like a top and driven off.
Then a lead soldier mold stood out.
Then 1ead poured in torrents
out of the one spot not man.
Then a ditto sheet with a woman
stylused on it and a storm of paper dittos
poured out into the wind
and were carried helplessly away.
Then there was a bitter silence.
Then God was flung out bruised,
spot not man and the silence was
like the quiver of pressure needles.
Then God came flinging out again,
but tore bloody headed back in,
and the silence was like the fall
of a hot star across an atmosphere.
Then an arm came hurling out
and grabbed a thorn bush fiercely
to keep from being sucked back in.
Then a head shot out and the arm
snagged it, dropped it, snagged
the body hurtling after it, put
a man together who made a
terrifying leap into the one spot
not man anymore and was hurled
back on his haunches where he
breathed until his rage calmed.
Then he put a question on a splint
and passed it through the one spot
not man and the splint was intact
in the silence, so he put an answer
on a sled, opened the doors to the
one spot and slammed in the sled,
and the answer skidded on gravel.
So he hurled himself into the spot
and was flung back like a ball again.
His arm went motionless, and his
head sank, and his body quieted
until time, not motion, filled
everywhere with growing shame.
"God made your arm, man."
came a voice, and the arm was still.
"God made your head, man,"
and the head was still. "God made

your whole body, man," and the
body was still. Then an arm came
out of the spot not man and tugged
at man. Nothing. Then a head
and a body came out and said
all together, "What is wrong, man?"
Then the sleeping man leaped up
and grabbed what had come out
of the spot not man, and there was
 a wrestle then a stunned stop.
The sleeper looked and saw this
was not the one spot not man
he wrestled with, and the one spot
not man was now empty,
could no way more be enticed
out from where it wished to be.
The other stood fiercely waiting.
The sleeper said, "We're too alike.
We're alike that we were made.
We're alike that we get turned
on and off like gas, on and off
like wind, like drubbing rain."
Then their rages calmed and the
sleeper said, "I'm empty." And the
other said, "I know a poem." And
The sleeper said,. "With rain and
scorching wind it it?" And he said,
"Yes, ladled from sun to moon to
sun." And the sleeper said, "It is a
solace." And the other, "Yes, it is."

VII RELAY
I said:
This parable.
A woman fenced a section of rich land
with electric barbed wire.
This will be called god's land, she said.
Its furrows were brown hair
on a running boy and she loved them.
The cottonwoods were girls.
The bean crop was a schoolyard of both.
It is god's land, she said.
She shot the first intruders with rock salt.
They forgot their pain and came back.

She killed them with a shotgun
saying, it is god's land
where we live the time until death calls
us home to a true home.
She ordered a vial of male sperm
saying, reach it over the fence
on a fishing pole. I will attach payment
to the pole when I have the sperm.
They came no closer.
She put the sperm in her cavity
and had a god's child
whom she raised on god's land,
teaching him, we must live god's land
until death calls us home.
The smell of great famine came through
the fence, so she and he took bean
seeds and watched the wind,
and when it turned, they threw the seed
 onto the wind to carry to the land
not god's to be planted there.
She put a sack on him for his wet dream
and sold the sperm over the fence
on a fishing pole to replenish the stock
she had depleted.
When the sound of war came
she plowed the beans under, removed
the fence, brought in rubble she strewed
beside the serpentine road she cut
through the section, and the armies roared
through the worthless ground.
Then she waited shrewdly, and they
roared back through the useless ground.
She buried the casualties outside god's land.
Then he and she cleaned the rubble
and cut the furrows brown as the hair
of boys and planted cottonwood girls.
But he loved the way,
so she took half the section and made
terrain for combat and there
fought mock battles with him at night
after tending god's land by day.
She drove him out. He drove her out.
She surrendered. He surrendered.
But in the day they grew their crop of beans,
and when the smell of famine came
threw seeds on the back of the wind,

and when the sound of any war came
She died and went to her true home,
and he could not propagate.
They could not reach a woman on a pole
over the fence for him, and no one
 but gods could walk upon his land.
He poured his seed upon the ground
and up came weaker beans.
He splashed his seed on the cotton woods,
and the hair of their heads fell out.
When the armies came he demanded surrender.
They devastated god's land,
left him for the carrion crows.

I said to him:
These voices after life:
I was a suicide. I still am.
With sweet gas?
Yes. I went to sleep.
Your voice is the wind in bells.
It is a ratchet.
No. It has pink flares.
Yes. The mark of suicide.
Why did you?
I surprised lies.
Your voice is the wind in silver maples.
You do love sound.
Your voice has varied qualities.
It is a drop forge.
That will crush anything.
 It's what I did.
Why? The lies you came on?
No. I am the lie.
Your voice is a blue glass pitcher.
You love color.
You have a sensual voice.
 It is a hand adze.
For chipping off tree bark?
Yes. To remove protections.
What do you mean?
The lie. The lie is organic.
As life is?
Yes. As I made it. Yes.
It made you.

It seems so. But not close up.
Your voice is a tambourine.
What rhythm has it?
Elegiac with requiem kettledrums.
That is not beautiful.
It is. But it has fear to it.
I am a lie.
I hear bead strings rattling.
As in a doorway?
Yes. Because of people entering
They are leaving. Or they left me.
What do you mean?
I would not love them.
Why bead strings?
To keep out flies. The best way.
No love. No staying.
Yes. No contemplation.
Something for something?
Yes. That is life exactly.
Your voice is a ragtime sound.
Player piano? With wheezings?
 Yes. Mechanical rhythms.
For a nickel?
Yes. Sort of a throwback.
I get played. I play.
The lie?
Yes. I made it.
You accepted it.
It comes down to the same thing.
There isn't any other way?
No, there isn't.
Your voice tastes like chicory.
I drank tons of it.
Your voice tastes bitter.
I know I give to get.
Not one giving?
No. There is a touch of happiness.
You did it for that?
Yes. But not the suicide.
Was that pure giving?
Yes. But selfish. A contradiction.
That is a pure lie.
I was a poet. I still am.
I thought so.
I committed suicide too.
I knew that.

From the way I sensed your voice?
No. From just the metaphors.
The way I used them.
Partly. And the way you clung to them.
As if I dodged you.
No. You brought in betrayals.
Set you in betrayals?
Yes. Death of beauty stuff.
I saw flesh faces toward the end.
I need more.
They floated in my semi-consciousness.
The hands of Angelico's Christ Mocked?
Yes. That's keen. Exactly.
Tasty as a pink plum.
Yes. Disembodied. Flute solos.
You sense the betrayal.
Yes. But I'm not any way a Christ.
What do you mean?
He was tasty as a pink plum.
Yes. Underneath the torture things.
He saw through the blindfold.
The hands, the metaphors, just hung.
I was the opposite. I am.
I need more.
Pink as a plum on the surface.
And the world was winged cherubs.
Can you imagine emptiness?
Yes. You know I can.
A coffee mill that grinds it out?
An invisible spout.
Yes. With a soundless noise.
And an ordorless scent.
Yes. Positive negatives.
Under the pink plum of a Christ Mocked?
Exactly. The reverse of Angelico.
That's what you killed?
No. That's not killable. You know it.
The pink plum surfaces?
Yes. They are the only killables.
Then why are they betrayals?
They succumbed to my killing.
And you did not.
Not when the negatives are positive.
You must have great regrets.
It is a quiet torture.
You mean when you speak in metaphor?

Yes. When I see Angelico.
But those paintings really flake.
They do not in my mind.
There is something terrible in your voice.
Will you be a poet?
No. That is to get something for something.
You sensed my longing then?
That you could not kill yourself?
Yes. The coffee mill of nothing.
But that is not the terror in your voice.
Please stop there.
I can't. You put me in your metaphors.
I do not mock you
But I am with pink plum flesh.
But not as Christ mocked.
But you kill, you killed metaphors.
Please stop there.
I can come to real death
I cannot do it.
You can finish yourself for good.
I do not want you to go.
You are a poet.

I said to her:
These voices after life:
The passions do not stop.
No. They are limitless.
They are needles through me, each.
You were gentle.
I lived in a green sky place.
Near the sea, then?
Yes. With dunes with pampas grass.
You will not understand.
I saw the blood of coots and terns.
Something. But not havoc.
As in a city? No, I haven't.
Hatred as in burning tires.
As in photos?
Smells reach you, sweet smells.
As in decay?

28 Do you hear truths?

But there is some nighttime.
As in peace?
Then you feel pure passion.
I do not. Shall I try?
No. What else was near you?
A waterfall. Onto the beach.
The sand drank it.
No. I made changing beds.
Water on washing board rocks.
Yes. A sound of riffling.
A limitless sound.
In dry seasons and high surf, no.
I mean the passions.
Yes. Lights into lights, but dark.
They never blink?
Hardly. That might mean loss.
Do you hear truths?   #28
Yes. Pitched as fierce spotlights.
But black light?
Yes. Sometimes strobe, in strokes.
The murdered are the most passionate?
No. It is the women.
How is that so?
They seem never to have lived.
And they know it?
Yes. But it is not anger.
It must be grief.
It is like a demonstration.
Who is listening?
No one else listens.
Why are you here?
I heard you singing a ballad.
 Mary Hamilton?
Yes. It had every feeling.
 But limited?
Yes. And everyone was there.
 They are in the demonstration.
I cannot bear it.
There are not so many murdered.
More are raped.
It is pure pain.
Yes. There is no defense.
Ballads are a minute's cushion.
Yes. And everyone is there.
There are no cushions for a passion.
Oh, god, no, there are not!

Passions are limitless.
Yes. I am one now. Unavoidably.
The green sky is helpless.
Only the ballad is not.
The next is of eternal havoc.
Will there be time for a soft one.
Not if I begin the next.
If I sing one, will you listen?
I will have to.

Francis Patrick Sullivan (d. 1996) a Jesuit priest, taught in the Theology Department of Boston College. As a teacher and student of religious imagination, he published several books of poetry (among them *CREDO & Other Poems 1995*), two volumes of psalm translations, stories for the liturgical cycle, and as a Las Casas scholar, *Indian Freedom: The Cause of Bartolome de las Casas* (1995). He held a MacDowell Colony residency for poetry and worked with a subcommittee of the International Commission on English in the Liturgy on the preparation of a new liturgical psaltar.

Aileen Callahan teaches in the Fine Arts Department of Boston College. She received an M.F.A. in painting from Boston University and has held fellowships to Mexico (Escuela Nacional de Pintura y Escultura, Mexico City) and Italy and the Skowhegan School of Painting and Sculpture. Her murals and other works are in collections in the United States, Europe and Mexico.